RASTA TIME

by
KATHY ARLYN SOKOL

© Copyright 2022 Kathy Arlyn Sokol
All rights reserved.

No portion of this book may be reproduced in whole or in part, by any means whatsoever, except for passages excerpted for the purposes of review, without the prior written permission of the publisher.

For information, or to order additional copies, please contact:

Beacon Publishing Group
P.O. Box 41573 Charleston, S.C. 29423
800.817.8480 | beaconpublishinggroup.com

Publishers catalog available by request.

ISBN-13: 978-1-949472-54-7

ISBN-10: 1-949472-54-7

Published in 2022. New York, NY 10001.

Cover photo courtesy of Mitsuhiro Sugawara

First Edition. Printed in the USA.

©*Michael Hofmann*

RasTa Time

©Mitsuhiro Sugawara

Table of Contents

Introduction
Bob Marley Interview
Bob's Family and Friends
Alford Calman Scott
Antonio Gladstone "Gilly Dread" Gilbert
Stephen Marley
King Sporty
Edward Seaga
Rohan Marley
Julian Marley
Donisha Prendergast
Rita Marley
Epilogue

©Mitsuhiro Sugawara

INTRODUCTION

~*The Tale of the Dancing Girl*~

> *Everyt'ing in time, mahn*
> *Everyt'ing in time……*
> **Bob Marley**

Time is our deepest mystery, our greatest desire. Time, wherein we live our lives, imparts the value of our treasures, the measure of our ambitions. Time also poses a paradox — never enough hours in the day, yet we have too much time on our hands.

The further we measure out our lives in clicks of clocks and crossed-out days on calendars, trying to stay "on" or "ahead" of time, the less spontaneous our lives become; and all the while, we know that however far ahead of time we may get for now, time will reclaim us inevitably; our "time" will be "up."

But what if we lived in "deep" time, what Bob Marley called the mystic or what I call RasTa Time?

It was a pre-dawn Sunday morning in Lawrence, Kansas, in 1976 when I first listened to Bob Marley's music. Lawrence's motto 'from ashes to immortality' is perhaps prophetic considering my ongoing relationship with a man who has been dead now for nearly 40 years.

I was in the kitchen of the Casbah Café, a trendy restaurant in the back of a craft shop that catered to hippies, bikers and yuppies alike, where I worked part-time while attending university. While baking my weekly quota of secret-recipe New York Jewish cheesecakes Jerry Riley, the head chef, came in smiling cryptically, saying he had a surprise for me. He went over to slip a record on the turntable, put the needle in the groove. Bob Marley's *Rastaman Vibration* came roaring out of the speakers, filling the air with a new and immediate magic.

As the fragrance of cheesecakes baking in the black cast-iron stove wafted through the room, the music coursed through my body, and though just approaching 5am, I started dancing. But there was more to what I was hearing than truly new and heart-filling music. What drew me in deeper and called me to listen once more and then again, was the realization that each of those songs carried a message.

Simple lyrics that called one to look within awakened a new kind of consciousness, not just for me but also for millions of people around the world. Bob Marley through Reggae music challenged us to re-examine our values, priorities, and purpose.

RasTa Time

The Journey Begins

Fascinated by the emerging detente between China and America in the 1970s after decades of enmity, I felt that my purpose was to learn about China and its people, and so upon graduation with a degree in journalism, I pursued a master's degree in Chinese. At the same time, I was hired by the National Public Radio (NPR) affiliate in Lawrence, Kansas to work as an anchorwoman and interviewer.

One of my first features was a half-hour piece with Faubion Bowers, who had served as General Douglas MacArthur's aide-de-camp and personal interpreter at the onset of the American occupation of Japan. When MacArthur's General Headquarters had banned *kabuki*, today known worldwide for its stylized acrobatic dance and elaborate make-up and magnificent costumes of brocades and cloths of gold and silk, Faubion, who considered MacArthur "a cultural barbarian," came to its rescue.

General Headquarters believed the themes of Kabuki too feudalistic to be performed in the post-war effort to democratize Japan. Faubion had lived in Tokyo before the war, teaching at Hosei University from 1940 to 1941, and learned Japanese by attending matinees of Kabuki daily, believing it to be one of the highest art forms in the world. He left his position as MacArthur's aide and became chief censor of Japan's theater in 1947, when he began to rework and release the plays one by one. Today Faubion Bowers is known as *"The Man who Saved Kabuki,"* which is also the title of a book about him written by Shiro Okamoto. In 1985, he was decorated by the Emperor of Japan with the Order of the Sacred Treasure.

Faubion loved the interview I did with him for NPR, and soon we were dining together regularly as I listened to his stories of travel throughout Asia in the 1940s and watched some of the more than 50 shows he wrote and produced on Asian arts for television. One night, after a few glasses of wine and a particularly intense discussion on the attributes of Japan versus China, Faubion suggested that instead of going to China as a foreign correspondent—my long-held career objective— I should go to Japan, which better suited my disposition.

I knew nothing of Japan, spoke no Japanese, and had already applied for a position with AP in Beijing. But Faubion persisted. Soon after, I whimsically packed my bags, said goodbye to the radio station and all my friends in Lawrence, and

RasTa Time

flew into Tokyo in June of 1978 with a one-way ticket and 200 dollars in my pocket.

I spent the first few days pouring coins into a public telephone calling every news and broadcast organization in the yellow pages looking for work. When I obtained a job interview with the founder of ALC, Inc., Teramaru Hiramoto, who published a pioneering radio magazine called the *English Journal (EJ)*, I played my NPR piece on Faubion as a sample of my work. It turned out that Hiramoto was a great admirer of Faubion Bowers, and instantly hired me as an interviewer for the *EJ*. Even today, over 40 years later, I contribute to the magazine.

Courtesy Hideki Nakagawa

Bob Marley Tours Japan

Courtesy Shin Miyoshi

The day I heard Bob Marley was coming to Tokyo, I immediately took a train to the *EJ* office and asked the editor if we could feature Bob in the magazine. He had never heard of Bob Marley, nor had anyone else in the office! Which perhaps wasn't all that much of a surprise, since, as I soon learned, Marley wasn't then widely known in Japan, the biggest venues he played there holding no more than 2500 people. I pleaded with the editor and finally persuaded him that the interview would be important, and grudgingly he gave his permission. On Friday, April 6th, 1979, I headed off to the concert with an issue of the *EJ* packed in my handbag.

Kathy Arlyn Sokol

The friend I had arranged to meet in front of the venue, and who held the tickets, arrived late, so by the time we were at last inside, the concert was already underway. Bob was dancing across the stage singing *Positive Vibration.*

I was definitely picking up on Bob's positive vibration and wasting no time. I put my belongings on my designated seat and went to the side aisle, about midway from the stage to dance. Just as Bob finished the song, two ushers approached and told me to return to my seat. I politely declined. The next time they tried, there were three ushers with a new twist to the same message: either sit down, or they would have the manager come and escort me out. I explained in my elementary Japanese that Bob was my *kamisama*...like a god to me, and dancing was my way of praying to him. They left to get the manager.

The manager arrived and gave me one last warning before starting to lift me toward the door. Bob had just finished a rousing rendition of *Punky Reggae Party*, saw the commotion and then looked straight at me — I wasn't difficult to spot, since I was the only one standing and dancing — suddenly he shouted from the stage: "Are you ready?" I screamed: "Yeeeesssss!" And then he launched into

RasTa Time

Get Up Stand Up. Confused by the moment, the manager loosened his grip while I called to the crowd, "Minasan Tatte! (Everyone stand up!) People started rising everywhere and soon a swell of bodies was swaying to the syncopated reggae dance rhythms that were throbbing from the stage. The manager released me and walked away.

©*Mitsuhiro Sugawara*

After the concert I headed backstage, brandishing my copy of the *EJ*, but was refused entry by two black-suited Japanese youths who took their responsibility of guarding the door with supercilious pride and imperiously informed me that Bob was not granting any interviews in Japan. At that precise moment the door opened and out stepped a foreigner, with thick black wavy hair hanging down past his waist. He took one look at me and asked: "Are you the dancing girl?" I certainly was, I nodded; he said: "Get in here. Bob would love to meet you." The guy just happened to be Bob's road manager, Vivienne, who brought me backstage and led me to Bob's dressing room.

RasTa Time

What followed was so much like a dream that I can't recall who else was in the room, or what Bob was wearing, as he sat reflectively at the table and slowly turned his face upward toward me. All that I can remember in any detail is the quality of his smile, radiating genuine sincerity, and an almost palpable field of unconditional trust around me. His smile allayed whatever anxiety I might have had about this meeting. His intent gaze mirrored the deep wisdom he had accessed through decades of prayer and meditation through countless nights of reading the Bible and holding 'reasoning' sessions with his Rasta brethren.

Shyly, barely above a whisper, he told me that we had made some magic tonight and thanked me. What could he do for me, he asked; without a moment's hesitation, I requested an interview; he agreed. We arranged to meet on Sunday, April 8, his day off. Not more than five minutes had passed, but this was not the time of the ticking clock, it was an experience of duration in 'deep' time where moments are eternities.

In RasTa Time, I am still there.

I later arranged for the EJ's engineer and photographer, Haruki Oshindai, to join me for the interview. He met me in the lobby of the Shinjuku Sunroute Hotel and from there we headed to the road manager Vivienne's room, where we would do the interview. Oshindai who was hooked on Pink Lady, stared wide-eyed through the open doors along the corridor, gaping at all the Rastas with their cascading dreadlocks, moving about in rooms of reggae music at full volume. As we entered Vivienne's room, from the compact cassette player aside the bed came the voice of Bob Marley, singing the lyrics to *War*.

Oshindai, looking more and more bewildered, attempting to recover his professional demeanor, set up the Uher reel-to-reel recorder on the single bed. Shortly after we were set up, Bob Marley walked through the door and sat down in the only chair, in front of the desk that was cluttered with touring and scheduling papers, midst which an ashtray overflowed with cigarette butts. I took the only other space available in the cramped hotel room — on the floor at his feet.

RasTa Time

Once again I found myself in 'deep time'. Others in the room faded into another existence; the room itself lost all the qualities of contextual space as I gazed steadily on Bob Marley's finely sculptured and gentle face, my mind in awe at the edge of disbelief. Was I actually talking, face to face, with Robert Nesta Marley, the King of Reggae? With the man who had been my guiding light and philosophical mentor for so many years as I'd made my transition from Lawrence, Kansas — a small university town with a population that hit 30,000 only when school was in session and where I had a tight group of friends — to Tokyo, a megalopolis of some 12 million inhabitants and growing, all who seemed equally oblivious of my existence?

But Bob Marley had noticed me amidst the throng of his audience, now here I was sitting at Bob Marley's feet and holding a microphone up to Bob Marley's face, because Bob Marley himself had granted me an interview! It was surreal.

When I told him how truly magical the concert the other evening had been, Bob laughed shyly, bringing me once again under the spell of his complete candor. His answer to my first question as to what kept him going, set the mood for the next hour.

"The truth. It's the truth that keeps it going, you know, and what you believe in. And you know that you're doing it for a purpose, so you might find your whole self involved with it, you know. And that is it."

RasTa Time

I soon put my list of prepared questions aside and focused my attention on what this man was urgently trying to convey, so wisely and yet so simply. As the hour passed Oshindai grew ever more confounded by what Bob and I were talking about and seemed poised to turn off the tape recorder. I confided to Bob, "I don't think that they will ever use this interview, but that is not why I am here."

I had fought my own battle with the 'system,' as Bob called it, and I was there to find out if I was alone in my struggle. Bob graciously let me know I was not.

"We believe in life. Everybody, everybody have life, you know, but the thing about life is that up to now nobody know how to keep it, you know. And we feel like all the material things that this here world might possess, I mean, without life, you wouldn't have anything. But people tend to turn it the other way—put the material in front of life, you know what I mean? So you find that we have a rebellious thing going on there, because some people won't accept the material things in front of life, they prefer life. You know what I mean?

We feel like, we don't feel, we know that our creation on earth is not a mistake. But over the past years and hundreds of years, the teaching and all of that philosophy is kind of wrong, you know. So, we call the teachings and the wrong things the system, you know. Like what is forced upon you and not what you really want, you know."

This was no longer an interview; it was a once-in-a-lifetime encounter between two people from utterly different backgrounds who nonetheless shared a sense of truth, purpose and mission. I didn't want

RasTa Time

our time together to end, but it did — when it had, we hugged, and as he'd done from the stage, he looked straight at me; and then he said: "Do the right thing with this, mahn."

Vivienne witnessed this final exchange, and with a nod from Bob invited me to join the rest of the tour. I said good-bye to Oshindai, now more baffled than ever, and took the chair that Bob had vacated. I closed my eyes and fell into a trance-like state right there, listening to ramblings of patois — like a chant — of the Rastas, incomprehensible to my untrained ear. I never even went home for a change of clothes.

Bob Marley Interview
April 8, 1979
Tokyo, Japan

©*Mitsuhiro Sugawara*

KAS: When you came the other evening, people were allowed to be free again; everyone just let loose.

BM: That's good.

RasTa Time

KAS: Do you know that you do that to people?

Bob Marley: Turn them loose? No.

KAS: You don't know.

BM: Not really. (Shyly laughing). You know the way I feel that is…but I was wondering if this is the way that they're going otherwise. Cause I was hoping… they seemed to be having a good time.

KAS: They were having a real good time. Do you usually do this? Do you get the same reaction out of people that you got the other evening?

BM: Sometimes you know. Sometimes.

KAS: It's the energy. What feeds you? What keeps it going?

BM: The truth. It's the truth that keeps it going, you know, and what you believe in. And you know that you're doing it for a purpose, so you might find your whole self involved with it, you know. And that is it.

KAS: *I've been accused of reading too much into the lyrics, into the words of the song, because I listen to them and I hear things like, "Get up, stand up for your rights," you know. And people say to me that that's not the purpose of the music. Do you have a message in your songs?*

BM: The purpose of the music is to get up, to stand up for your rights, of course, you know. I mean, there's no way that you can really sidetrack the truth and the reality of what's happening around the earth, you know. So the music, I'll do it …it is a music that can make you happy. You know. It can make you happy in a rebellious way, you know what I mean? If for the first time you might feel free for really express yourself in a, in a different way, you know. So the music, when you're really into it is because you're rebelling against the system, you know what I mean?

KAS: What system are you rebelling against?

BM: Well, what is happening now is that we believe in life. You know what I mean? We feel like, we don't feel, we know that our creation on earth is not a mistake. But over the past years and hundreds of years, the teaching and all of that philosophy is kind of wrong, you know. So, we call the teachings and the wrong things the system, you know. Like what is forced upon and not what you really want, you know.

You see, the newspapers and the media, you know, they don't really…the media is controlled everywhere, in every country. So, what the newspapers are saying is not what the people is really interested in.

KAS: It's something that somebody wants to tell us, but it doesn't have any meaning.

BM: Yeah, it's just a waste of time. You know, so that it keep on going and it keep on going. Say if you get tapped, you might get interested, start listening, start reading a lot, hoping that one day they will say the truth. But the truth is that if they say the truth then all governments on earth will have to break down, and all propaganda. So they have to keep on feeding the propaganda so that them can have a system going.

But we like people, you know what I mean? We're not looking at ourselves as musicians and all that; we're checking ourselves as people. And we feel like if somebody going to force down something on you, we don't really see life in that sense, you know, just accepting what is happening and…cause we know that there's somebody make the rules, you know, and at the time that the people make the rules they didn't have to be right. So if they are wrong today they should accept that they are wrong, you know.

KAS: The earth is flat. This is a fact. Right? Everybody believed this for so long…the earth is flat. And then all of a sudden the truth comes. Hey, wait a second…

BM: The earth is round. (laughter)
So just like today, you know, you find a man. Everybody, everybody have life, you know, but the thing about life is that up to now nobody know how to keep it, you know. And we feel like all the material things that this here world might possess, I mean, without life, you wouldn't have anything. But people tend to turn it the other way—put the material in front of life, you know what I mean? So you find that we have a rebellious thing going on there, because some people won't accept the material things in front of life, they prefer life.

Not just one individual. Because it's like politics…if five people say there is something that is right and five people say it is not right and one says its right, although the one who says its right is right, the five people that say it is wrong, they have more power, you know, because it's like against odds, you know. So it's something like that today. *(laughter)*

KAS: *The other evening I walked into the concert and I stood up, and I was dancing on the side. This was at the beginning and I was just dancing and really just getting into the music, and they tried to make me sit down. These people came and they forcefully pushed me and said, "Sit down!" And I said, "Hey, this is Bob Marley and I'm not bothering anybody, I'm standing here and I'm*

dancing. And they couldn't accept that. They were, "sit down, sit down." And then you came out with Get Up Stand Up and then everybody just moved. There was no way to keep them down. But because I was one I couldn't do that.

BM: Yeah, but if everybody did then the little three or the four that come and tell you 'sit down' have no power, you know. So just like today, if the people realize that life is more than just working for the next man until you retire on pension. I mean, you know, working is good, you know, but we have to have something else…

KAS: That keeps it inside you.

BM: Yes. (laughter) Have to really respect what we feel of this atmosphere, I mean, you know, love and respect creation, you know. And then you start search, and you will find Rastafari.

You might have some people who say they are leftist or rightist or labor party or any political type of things that people tend for really looking for the answer, but the answer is Rastafari.

Ras means head, Tafari means creator. Now… the people, natural people, we're not talking about government who control the coming in and the going on. We're talking about natural people in the street. Natural people are ready to accept the truth, but they need help, you know. And they can't get their help because the government never study these things. They study how to manipulate people and how to stay in power.

And at the same time, it's not because he want to tell you to sit down. Because if he never have the job and there wasn't someone watching him, then he might lose his job. (laughter) If somebody wasn't watching him, they would just leave you alone, you know. But somebody tell him, all right, these people mustn't dance and they mustn't jump up, and we put you in charge to make sure that they don't do that, alright? Yeah, okay, sir, I'm programmed. And they say, sit down, sit down, sit down, and you say, no, and him say, yes, you have to sit down and you say, no.

KAS: But there's some reason the government is the government. Why are we allowing these people in control to control us without saying, "hey wait a second, this isn't really what I want." Why do we allow it?

BM: Well, you see, because our greatest enemy is fear, you know. And again until you know the truth, you can't really know what is happening. Because if nobody know about Rasta, then everybody will be talking about God, you know, and God say him will return in a new name which when he come back is God. He will have a new name with the same meaning as God.

KAS: Great God is a living man…

BM: Yeah, can't tell you that you're not living and God create life, you know. So, that's why I say. Why them allow these things to happen is because it is forced upon them. Guns, bayonets, rumors, I mean, it couldn't be worse.

KAS: I awoke in a curfew, great god I was a prisoner, too. Are we all inmates in a societal prison?

BM: We're all prisoners. I mean, our mind is free and we might can move, but we're still prisoners. This is a curfew. I mean, I could not go anywhere and anyplace and do anything that I want to do which I know is right. You know, some place the right thing is wrong and nobody care about that. And they're going to tell you that this is the law. And then who make the law? You can never find the people who make the law because these people is the devils.

They make this law that you must always live, work for the man and then you die. And his thing is, oh, somebody else will come and do the same work as long as you keep dying and babies born and they come and do the same thing and everybody just go around in this great machine you know. They don't care, but God care 'cause Ras Tafari don't like that. But rather than to use force, Ras Tafari can't use force, so you have to use what is inside of you, you know. Some people find satisfaction, material satisfaction, because maybe during the small days they used to suffer so when they get big now they start getting "buy this," the mind stop think, the whole thing is survival—where are we going to sleep tonight, where are we going to eat tomorrow, you know.

The people have to accept the truth, and not even the people because until the whole teaching come that everyone will hear and can pick for themself before any good will ever happen.

But everybody bowing to nuclear powers and big war and temptation and war, and you find people get coward because oh, my country going to fight war anytime the devil going to tell you come, you have to go and fight.

Now, you might say, well, you might check him and say, 'well, this guy, he was a baby, right? Mother bring him up in love, tender care, him start creep, then him walk. And him go to school and then him start grow up—let him start think for himself now. And then the things that they teach you to think about is not good. And if you don't know that it is not good from early, later it going to be too late. Because you can't just bend an old tree, might as well chop it down, you know. But if it's a young tree, you can steer the young tree.

So, the people is not really, I mean, Jahveh say, a new generation have to have to come, you know. Because it's like this generation has drinked, drinked the whole wine already and are drunk. So, it's only their children could get the truth because…it's not their fault, you know, it's the devil in him, the devil bring it down, you know.

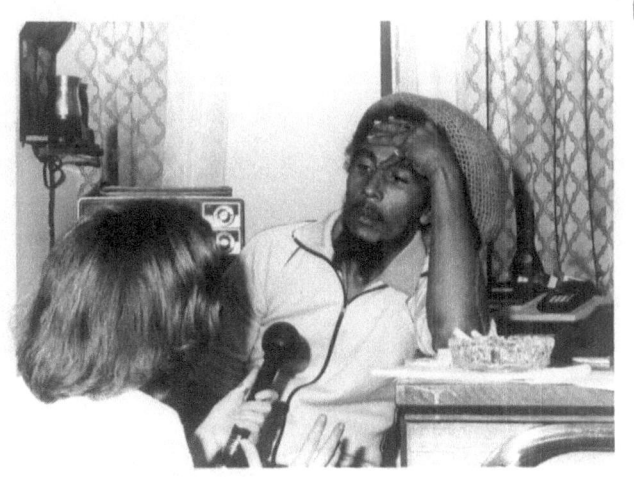

KAS: So, how do you raise the consciousness?

BM: There's only one way. Ras Tafari, and the one has to have that truth within them, and the respect for life, you know. If everyone feel like life is not important, because that's how them feel that life is not important, but we know that life is important, and we can be traitors to god, you know. We have to really defend the truth.

KAS: Is Sheriff John Brown a real figure or is he symbolic of any oppressive...

BM: Yeah, oppression. (laughter) Sheriff John Brown, yeah, you know. The whole oppression…….

Kas: To not let the seeds of dissent be planted…

BM: Yeah, him say kill them before they grow, right? That mean if you start say…you might start read the lyrics which are simple lyrics, you know…get up stand up for your rights, you're going to have someone come tell you, no don't deal with that, you know. So, it's like every time we plant a seed, they say kill it before they grow because if you get to understand the truth, then it will be all over.

KAS: Once we begin to understand the truth, then this whole society that we've created for ourselves no longer has any meaning.

BM: No, it don't have any meaning, not no real meaning. It's just a big pretensive thing going on…

KAS: Marijuana in Japan is something that you don't talk about. In Jamaica, marijuana is

something that really has strength. (Yeah, mahn.) What is the strength of marijuana? What does it do for you?

BM: Marijuana is a great…we call it the herb. It's the healing of the nation, you know. Well, we look at it in this simple way, like: first them say, why the law or why the government don't want the people to use this plant? Now this is not something that somebody make. This is something that grow—a natural, harmless thing, you know. If you step on it, it never hurt no one.

But the thing is, it's psychological trick. I mean, it's an international one, too. All of them gather themselves together to fight against the herb. Why? If all people on the face of the earth should, not even smoke it, you know, but just, just even see it natural like, see it, you get used to it. Everybody will think one way. You understand?

RasTa Time

Now if you have Japan thinking or Jamaican thinking like...I mean, everybody would have to be thinking like the Jamaican right now.

KAS: It's not that everyone has to be thinking like a Jamaican. I think the marijuana allows certain inhibitions to falter, to go away and that's the fear is that it allows you to be ….

BM: Yourself. And if you be yourself, then there's a lot of people are going to be themself. And if I be myself and you yourself, there's no way there can be any negative thing in between because we are all ourselves and we respect one another for ourself. But as long as there is something there that we can't get through to one another, that is a problem, cause you know what I mean. You have Russia and America fighting a propaganda war that is about to come out one day, that maybe will never take place. (laughter) So everybody is sitting and waiting around for that day and meanwhile, they're dying. And new babies are born and so all of that is nothing. Foolishness.

KAS: It goes around and around…

BM: They try to take us around and around and tell you. The solution to the herb problem is herb. If everyone can have it…we're not saying everyone is going to smoke, you know. But if it were something that one could have in one's house like flowers. I mean, it would be nice…

KAS: Nice to look at. Nice to smell.

BM: Nice to live in. It would be nice. But until that day it will be our problem. Because the thing is in this confusion and this confusing world is the man who live out in the country have can think. Because living in the city where you have television and radio, the air condition, the car, the train, everything, there's no where you can think. So, you know, God give you one gift. He give you herb. (sound of taking a drag) and cure what is going on. You can turn them off. And deal with yourself.

RasTa Time

***KAS:** ...and deal with that that is really around us. All of this is created for some purpose, I don't know why.*

BM: Foolishness, bad, dust, just vanity.

***KAS:** Is it inbred, have we been indoctrinated to believe that this right, and that we need it for our existence?*

BM: You know, they can get the board and everything, and can make these things, and people use their mind. But when the people live without these things, you know, they live stronger. They're only there for the money trick. It's just dead. It's dead.

'Cause you know what I mean if everybody was taking a little drag all the minds would communicate one way. But this world is a confused world. Everybody have a different confusion going on in their head, you know. Somebody have a problem somewhere which don't really exist because whatever excuse you have to make a feel a problem and the problem is a material problem and then your flesh must suffer for it. You know what I mean? I really hate that.

KAS: A couple of years back somebody tried to shoot you down. What was that all about?

RasTa Time

BM: The devil, you know what I mean? Just a devil work because a man like me now if them can get rid of me easy, maybe some guy figure it will be better for them.

KAS: Who was the guy?

BM: The devil.

KAS: The devil?

BM: Yeah. Him have people that him use all over. I mean, the devil is like you say—the devil is a harm and a force that wound people, you know. It's just negative force, you know. Some people don't even know that they're working for the devil, but the things that they do is working for the devil. You know what I mean? And the devil always wants your life. So him want to prove God, say God wrong, you know.

So why would someone want to kill someone? So someone might say why did God make I and I have to die? If God create you I don't see why…anything that God give, Him don't take it back. Him give us the sun and Him give us the moon, you know, and He never take it back. Same He give us life and He not going to take it back. But the devil always want it.

And then when the devil want it, new babies born because God cannot be defeated. So, might kill our flesh, then 50 more flesh come. So they say, all right, birth control, I mean, the government we have to find a way to kill off all these people; we have to find a way. So them say, birth control, but that don't work neither because you might have birth control here but over there people having millions of children and ….I mean, there is no way that they can defeat God which is Ras Tafari.

Him rule the yard. But you see God is not a dream nor like of the sky. He's a natural; Him have a natural house that Him live in. Yeah. And He can do many….I mean, He's God. Great. Heavy. Him don't have to make Himself invisible to please nobody. Him is God, Him is the first visible, and then He make all people can see him through the creation.

RasTa Time

©*Mitsuhiro Sugawara*

KAS: The only thing I really know about Jamaica is reggae music. How reflective of Jamaica is reggae music? Is it what is happening there?

BM: Reggae music is what's happening in the people, man. Jamaica is like any other place—government, same thing. The only difference with Jamaica now is because the people are more rebellious, you know, them really rebellious. They're Rasta.

When Rasta, when Rastaman just find themself, the government say anybody who is with them or toward them, shoot them down. You know. And all these Rasta get a hard time. Whenever you're looking at a prison, he's always Rasta. And every black man in Jamaica is a Rasta, so there's no way that you can stop them because the only thing that can stop them is to drive fear into people...before I even get to know this fate, I didn't even try to know it, you know. But it is something that is just in me and I, that means I must live it. Because when he's a Rasta, you're not treated like not like an ordinary citizen, you're really looked to as an outcaste like, you know what I mean. Which is true because we're not really with the system.

KAS: Just flick it off.

BM: Yeah, but we don't care. Because that is good. Because what is happening now is that we're changing from this and we don't want them to accept us because we're not looking for acceptance. We're looking for growth. You know, the more people who get to know the truth is the more...and that is it.

KAS: and it will take hold.

BM: You can't stop it. Everything is in prophecy. This is the generation that see God. This is the people. This is the generation. That mean over the whole earth. This generation of people seek the truth. That is what is happening right now. No government or no nuclear weapon nor nothing at all can stop it. You know. Because everybody break it down.

Oh, the man whose dealing with this was a baby. All along he was a baby. Fifty years ago he was a baby. I mean, where him get all of this great knowledge that him tell us today of some strange doctrine. Ras Tafari is the truth, you know, and it's proof. I mean, it's the truth. I'm proof. Everybody have the truth, you know. And everybody want to live good. We know. We feel it.

KAS: We want to, yeah, but it's going to take somebody to stand up. And to say, okay, this is what I want...

BM: It gonna grow. You see, it soon be done. Because the last thing them try is this thing in Ethiopia to really change the people, but it educate the people more. Because the people might say, now, all right, you say His majesty, His majesty as someone who you can't see.

I mean, it's just like a record. Right? I'm in Jamaica and I make this record and it may be good for people and everybody get it, but I don't have to be there. So, it's just like the teachings of His Majesty, the philosophy, the ways of life, the example that Him set, that man should follow.

No president, no prime minister, no kings, none of them ever deal with it like that. It is something that I can't even explain myself. I have to just live with it. I mean, live on, try to stay with life because every day they want your life.

Yeah, you know what I mean. Some people say that His Majesty is just a man. But we know that His

Majesty is more than man, He is God. And the teachings of this man...some people like yogi, some people like Buddha, some people like all of them things, but out of all of them things the only true one is His Majesty own, you know. The Christ.

KAS: It means something that can give you the truth; it means that it is there for you to see.

BM: For all people, all people. Why are all these people coming up today? Anywhere you're going you see Rasta. Somebody want to know what you're saying. Some people don't even know they are Rastas, but them is Rastas. Everywhere you going you meet them. So everything is coming, you know. Look at more, man, look at more. And the whole thing will all be over 'cause it will be. It won't last. That is all, man. Everything is going to come to an end.

You see when one ready, there's a lot of people who's ready. But this revolution will not be televised, it shall be telepathic, you know. That mean we don't expect the newspapers to promote Rasta.

'All right, people, if you don't do this, there is no other way. There is no other way, but this way.' Nobody going to say that because, I mean, this world is so in league with countries, in league with one another that if Russia is going to help Jamaica, then Jamaica has to be socialist, right? If America is going to help Jamaica, then Jamaica has to be capitalist. There is no way you can be Rasta and you get any help. You dig? So, Rasta we don't have no great guns or atomic weapon, but we have the truth.

RasTa Time

We don't care about who bring guns or who throw bombs. We don't care about that. We are Rastas, and if we have to throw bombs, too, we will. You understand? But when they're going to throw bombs, we say all right, we are capitalists, so we're going to throw bombs because who make the bombs? The capitalists make the bombs, so if you are going to throw bombs…

KAS: and it employs lots of people.

BM: So we don't want to be like that. We prefer just live like real people and suffer every day until these people grow. And it will be all over very soon. You know, most people go to school and learn different, different things. It's time other people go to school and learn of Rastafari. You see. And that is what's happening.

Noah had three sons. Noah. That's history. When mankind was lost and him never know who his father. History show that Noah had three sons: Ham, Shem and Jahvet, you know. Ham is a black man, Shem is dusky, and Jaffet is a white man. So, all these three people come from one father. That's how we know that Ras Tafari will reach everyone.

KAS: The other evening you were directing energy. You were letting it go. I just put my hand out and I could feel it.

BM: If you're with it, you can feel it, you know. It's a lot of people ready now. I mean, this is the generation that see God. This is the last days. God say Him shall return within 2000 years. This is one thousand nine hundred and seventy-nine. I mean, 21 years with 2000 years close. Him never say that He was coming at the end of 2000 years. Him say that he was coming within. And of all the people on the face of the earth telling you about God today in reality, and I can assure you him is Rastaman.

RasTa Time

And God never make a mistake. We don't have to have no great education to know God because education don't teach you about God anyhow. We don't have to be liars, lawyers, nor teachers to tell you about god, because God feed you with inspiration until you go and tell the people, you know.

KAS: Maybe burnin and a looting. Burning all illusions?

BM: All illusion. Madness. You have to burn everything. I mean, it shall be a new world. Cause this world shall be passed away.

Let me tell you something…that if President Carter get up tomorrow and say, "You know that Rastas are really right, all of America become Rastas because then the police and the soldiers and all of them would have to allow the people to be what they want to be.

A man like me now going to a certain place you have people watch you. The first thing they might figure is a bandit…Him not looking at you. First thing them say is, "watch him." So you feel this vibe, and you…say you deal with it and then come on back. Now them people figure them don't know what is happening, them don't even know who was there a while ago. I mean, they didn't even talk to the one to find out if that one would have anything good to say. See? Them never find out that, them just judge you right away. Oh…you know?

KAS: Maybe I shouldn't think of you as a Messiah, but it's the Word, and you are bringing that to the people. And that is what I feel in your music…

BM: Yeah, it's not everybody will be there. It's only some, but the whole thing can be one again.

RasTa Time

*Do the right thing
with this mahn,
do the right thing...*
            Bob Marley

Kathy Arlyn Sokol

©*Mitsuhiro Sugawara*

RasTa Time

Making the Tape

Even though the interview format was a significant departure from the *English Journal's* normal fare, they allowed me to publish it. My idea was to introduce Bob Marley to the Japanese public by producing a short primer of reggae, Rasta and Marley's philosophy of life. After weeks of listening to the interview again and again while sitting under the trees at Inokashira Koen, on the train from Kichijoji to Shibuya, or at night in my bed, I crafted an 11-minute piece.

I had approached Toshiba EMI — Bob's distributor at the time — for permission to use some of the songs, and was told that it would cost me 200,000 yen per minute, which was out of the question. I then called Chris Blackwell, the man who 'discovered' Bob Marley and released his albums on the label he had established, Island Records. Chris was eager to get publicity in Japan for Bob, and for reggae, so offered me free use of the music if in exchange I would interview another of his artists, Robert Palmer, when he arrived in Japan the following month. Of course I agreed, and within a week I received a letter signed by Chris Blackwell that I was to bring to Toshiba, informing them of his decision.

Kathy Arlyn Sokol

Move to Kyoto

In 1980, I began a new job as editor-in-chief of *The Embassy Journal*, a magazine that ostensibly would feature in-depth interviews with ambassadors from around the world who represented their countries in Tokyo. It was exhilarating. I was earning big money while being chauffeured around Tokyo in a Mercedes Benz equipped with a telephone — very rare in those days — driving from one meeting to the next.

I should have realized that something was amiss, however, when I was handed a fat envelope at the end of each month and wasn't even required to sign a receipt. One afternoon the founder of the magazine invited me to lunch to explain his true intentions in establishing the magazine. He picked me up in his Rolls Royce right outside the office whose meeting room featured a 5-meter-high golden Buddha in a glass case filled with 10,000-yen notes. Over lunch, he explained to me that the magazine was just a cover to create a base for his becoming a power broker for Japan, his specific interest being South Africa. This was 1980 and apartheid was still the rule of the land, and this man was trying to encourage Japan to establish full diplomatic relations despite the U.N. supported sanctions in place against South Africa. Right then I decided no matter how much money I was making it was not worth supporting this unethical endeavor, and I quit.

Soon after that, I moved from Tokyo to Kyoto, to start a new life there with W. David Kubiak, known for creating Japan's first 'livehouse,' Jittoku.

I had actually been to Jittoku before I met David. My first summer in Japan, I had hitchhiked down to Kyoto with a friend, and we were told we had to visit this truly historic landmark, remade from an old sake brewery wedged in the backstreets. On the night we found Jittoku, by the time we finally arrived, the evening's performance had already ended, so we just sat down to have a drink. When only a few people remained in the place, the staff put Bob Marley's *Exodus* album on and turned it up. We all jumped to our feet and started dancing. Though I was barely able to speak a word of Japanese, I saw now and understood what Bob meant when he said that reggae music knew no color, no race, no barriers.

Lost Tape

David and I planned to live in India for a while, so we packed everything for the shift, including my cassette copy of the Bob Marley interview. Since the copy was for transcribing only, and had been recorded on the cheapest of tapes, I simply tossed it into one of the boxes, knowing that ALC had the original Uher recording. The boxes went into storage in a friend's barn at his horse ranch up in the mountains north of Kyoto and stayed there for many years.

RasTa Time

Meanwhile, we lived between India and the States, but with the introduction of FedEx and fax machines, I continued contributing to the *English Journal*. In 1985, ALC's President, Hiramoto Terumaro, paid all expenses for our return to Japan, and although we decided to live in Kyoto I often traveled to Tokyo to meet with the president and the *EJ* staff. On one visit, I asked if I could make a copy of my interview with Bob Marley. I was informed that the tape had accidentally gotten lost when ALC had moved its office from Hiroo to Eifuku in the Tokyo metropolis. I simply couldn't believe it. I immediately began searching through the stacks that ALC had of literally hundreds and hundreds of files containing copies of all the interviews that the *English Journal* had ever published — 6 interviews per month, every year since the magazine started in 1974.

I continued the search each time I went to Tokyo. Sometimes Oshindai-san, now an executive at the company, would give me a hand sifting through the files while we reminisced about that April 1979 Sunday morning we spent with the King of Reggae. But despite our efforts, the reel was never found. I knew it was a lost cause and reminded myself that the memory of the experience was the important thing. I also took some solace in knowing that I still had my cheap cassette copy in some box somewhere amongst the piles of boxes that we'd moved into our Kyoto home. But like the reel tape, the cassette never surfaced.

Until one day 30 years later, in 2009, when David was in the backyard shed going through a box of miscellaneous tapes, mostly old audiocassettes. He sorted through them, reading the labels — Sting, Milt Jackson, B. B. King, Jimmy Cliff — names of people I had interviewed in the past. Then he called me outside and tossed me a cassette scribbled with what looked like the letter B… and possibly a scrap of a y scrawled across it in red oil pencil. We only had a CD player, so I put the tape aside praying that I'd find our old Sony cassette player/recorder stored away in some other box.

When I came across the player a few months later, I ran to get the mysteriously labeled tape, took a few deep breaths and put it in to play. Out of the far past came Bob Marley's voice saying to me back then, in another moment of RasTa Time: *"…it is the truth that keeps it going and what you feel inside, and to know you are doing it for a purpose."*

RasTa Time

As I listened to Bob speaking to me again after decades, I could not help but wonder: what was the purpose of my finding this tape only after 30 years?

Was it just a coincidence that Chris Blackwell of Island Records was now backing a film on Marley, to be directed by Jonathan Demme, who was planning to have Bob himself narrate, by collecting interviews and video footage of Marley from around the world?

Was it just a coincidence that my son Kazu knew a talented engineer, Kondo Tadashi, who worked with Soft Tribe, one of Kyoto's best-known underground bands, and was willing to transfer the tape to CD for me?

Was it just a coincidence that one day Kazu's best friend from high school, Ijichi Ryo, came to the house with Ayumu Takashi, a best-selling author with his own publishing company and a keen interest in Jamaica, where he sponsors a music school?

There is an expression in Japanese, *"guzen ga nai,"* which translates, "There are no coincidences."

When Ayumu stepped through the entryway of my Kyoto house, he apologized for only being able to visit for a few minutes as he was expecting friends from Tokyo to momentarily arrive. As we talked, Rasta minutes passed and passed, until Ayumu finally contacted his friends and asked them to come meet him at my house.

Drinks and snacks were served, the minutes turned to hours and we talked well into the Rasta night about Ayumu's travels around the world, mostly focusing on his time in Jamaica. As a parting gift, I asked him if he would like to hear the *EJ* excerpt of my interview with Bob Marley. His answer was a wide-eyed "Yes!" He listened intently while reading the Japanese translation that had appeared with the English transcript in the September 1979 issue of the *EJ*. The 11-minute piece came to an end, Ayumu paused for a moment, and then proposed publishing the interview as part of a book on Bob Marley.

RasTa Time

With events being organized around the world to honor the 30th year of Bob Marley's passing, it seemed the perfect time to release not just the excerpted version, but the classic interview in its entirety, which had never been heard by anyone but me.

Scheduling Time

To make a book that would be relevant today, we decided to interview some of Marley's friends and family. So interviews had to be scheduled, hotels booked, tickets purchased. In preparation, I paid a visit to the Jamaican Ambassador, Claudia Barnes, to discuss the book project. She was a big fan of Bob's, and never traveled to a new posting without her Bob Marley CD collection in her carry-on. She had been at the One Love Peace Concert in Jamaica in 1978 and spoke about it with deep nostalgia.

Courtesy Jack Low

Bob Marley had participated in that concert to help quell the civil war environment that had intensified in Jamaica during a particularly bitter political campaign for prime minister, between socialist-leaning Michael Manley and US-allied Edward Seaga. During a powerful performance of *Jammin'*, Bob Marley called Seaga and Manley onstage, much to their surprise, while he went into trance, chanting about uniting in love under the moon.

Watching the blurred and poorly filmed archival footage of the event, you can feel the heft of Bob's prayer that music could temper the two rivals' belligerence. He clasped their hands together in a symbol of unity, continuing to chant while holding out his other hand in a gesture of love to the electrified crowd of 30,000 fans. Perhaps the moment did not have a long-lasting impact, but it gave the world a taste of how music can merge with politics to transform the lives of the people, even if only for a key moment.

In another coincident moment, when I met with Ambassador Barnes the following week to introduce her to Ijichi Ryo, the producer of the book project, she and I did a miracle kind of double-take when she entered the room wearing the same red-and-black Kashmiri pashmina shawl that I had over my shoulders. She had gotten hers in Belgium and I bought mine in Srinagar. The probability of such a thing happening was incalculable; the augury of it was apparent to us both. We took it as a positive sign — an omen even, that linked us together in some higher way — and that bode well for the book.

ALFORD CALMAN SCOTT

The Ambassador told me about a Rasta friend of hers from Jamaica who had lived in Tokyo for 30 years, named Alford Calman Scott. Better known as Scottie, he had known Bob in the early days, and the Ambassador thought that Scottie might be a good contact for me. She called him up, briefly explained my project and handed me the phone. We arranged to meet near Scottie's recording studio in Omotesando.

Kathy Arlyn Sokol

Courtesy Alford Calman Scott

Scottie, a musician in Jamaica with a hit single *Devil in the City* released in 1976, used to hang out at Bob's house on 56 Hope Road after the other Rasta brethren had departed for the day.

They would sit around the fire in the yard, Bob strumming the guitar and Scottie singing back-up harmonies to songs like *Could This Be Love?* before Bob went into the studio to record them with the Wailers. Scottie had intended to join Bob on tour in Japan in 1978, but at the last moment the visa did not come through; Bob got on the plane without him, promising to promote him when he returned to Jamaica. But Scottie never saw Bob alive again.

RasTa Time

In 1981, Scottie ventured to Japan on his own. He had landed a gig at a club in Roppongi, the then ritzy section of Tokyo that was trying to popularize Reggae music. Although Reggae was a world craze, Japan was a little slow in catching on; at Scottie's band's first show, there was no one in the audience. Refusing to play another night to empty chairs, Scottie asked the manager to take them to where the young kids hung out; he wound up at the Tokyo landmark, *Hachiko* in Shibuya. It was a hot, sultry summer night, so the Rasta boys doffed their tams and let their dreadlocks loose, the sight of which created a fright among the crowd; the usually bustling square was empty within minutes. But as the band eased into the reggae beat, by ones, by twos, by threes and more, the crowd returned.

Kathy Arlyn Sokol

BOB MARLEY'S FAMILY & FRIENDS INTERVIEWS

RasTa Time

Courtesy Alford Calman Scott

Kathy Arlyn Sokol

©*W. David Kubiak*

Alford Calman Scott Interview

KAS: *Bob Marley's message has spread all around the world. What do you think his message was?*

Alford Calman Scott (ACS): Life.

Japan, for example, has its culture and we have ours. Japan is a technology country and they invent a lot of things. But that is not the order of the day. You have a life that cannot be invented. You understand me? So, the movement of the people, as Bob sings, is to find out your true self and what you are here for.

But man cannot find his spirit. You are not here just to wear clothes and eat food and work and buy a video and watch a movie. You are here for a very special reason. You must find that reason. In a country like Japan there are so much commercial things. But if you discover the real life, you will find out that silver and gold will vanish away but a good education will never decay. (Laughs.) You may have a new car, but a car can't serve more than a certain age. The furniture cannot serve forever, not even your body can serve forever. So, what is life then?

RasTa Time

KAS: Could you talk about the world of Rastafari in which Bob lived?

ACS: Well, Bob Marley is a simple man who came to be so powerful that his life's work resembled that of Jesus Christ's. I saw in him a need to do that kind of work. I never saw it when I was young as I see it now.

There was no time. When we could see the fate of Rastafari, we Rastas knew that we were going in the right direction, but the citizens of Jamaica weren't with us. We were all by ourselves; so all Rasta people united and helped one another.

The younger set of people now they just see the style of Rasta, and it looks good, it's like a fashion. Many people grasp for the Rasta look, and they think if they wear the long hair they are in the same category as Bob Marley. But they do not stop to realize that behind it is a movement, and check to see what is at the root of the Rasta philosophy.

Like you will see a tree. The tree has leaves and branches but it has a root that push out these things. So we are coming from the roots. Those who just grasp for the look are like the leaves. (Laughs.) So, we cannot be angry and say, "Oh, you only like the leaves." Some will be like the leaves, some will be like the branch, and some will just love the tree.

For Rastas, the month that you were born is an indication of what you are capable of doing. Bob Marley, for example, was born under the sign of Aquarius, the water bearer. People born under this sign are givers who feed and provide for the people. Bob never took for himself; he always gave to others.

KAS: How did the Rasta community begin to grow in Jamaica?

ACS: Rastafarianism started long time ago. It began with the river Nile. A portion of the Nile River starts at Lake Tana in Ethiopia and as the Nile flowed, so flowed the knowledge of human civilization into the world.

If you read the Bible you will find that Ras Tafari is there. Ras means head, and Tafari means creator. Ras Tafari Makonnen is from the family of the Ras Tafaris. He descends from King Solomon and Queen of Sheba and took the name Haile Selassie the 1st when he was coronated in Ethiopia in 1930. The Ethiopian imperial line from the House of Solomon continued unbroken until 1974.

RasTa Time

The Rastafarians were in Jamaica from the time that the slaves were brought over. Some of the slaves ran away to the mountainous interior and established a free community in a place called Maroon Town. The Queen could not get them to surrender, and even today a piece of their land in western Kingston is not part of Jamaica. They survived by subsistence farming and never had to go under the wine press, working everyday for a master. These escaped slaves kept the customs and beliefs of their motherland, Africa.

Then in the 1920s Marcus Garvey, who was an educated man and schoolteacher, started to talk about Africa to Jamaicans. He talked of black pride, dignity and freedom from oppression and urged the black man to look to Africa for their king. Then when Ras Tafari became Emperor of Ethiopia in 1930 people started to listen to his message more carefully. They heard his words like a song, and the Rastafarian movement began to spread through the slums of Kingston. Garvey planned to buy seven miles of ships, which he called the Black Star Liner that would take us out of the West and back to Africa. But he could only afford one. (laughs).

They called the Rastas "bushmen" and all kinds of names. People tried to put fear into us about the Rastas, saying things like "they take away children and they don't bathe or wash their hair." Rastas washed with a fruit that has a seed and foams like soap when rubbed. They knew how to live off the land. Give Jah thanks and praise because he feed us with plentiful fruits, yams, coconuts, almonds....

As a Rasta you could never go into a regular store to buy things, so they used to take car tires to make their shoes. I come to Roppongi, the swanky district in Tokyo, and I see that they sell tire shoes for 35,000 yen. Onions used to come in big, meshed hemp bags and the Rastas used those bags to make clothes. Today clothes made out of hemp are the fashion. But in Jamaica at that time the Rastas were thought to be wearing garbage.

Rasta man survive because we have the sun, we have the water; we could live in the mountains because it was free. You couldn't run a fence around a mountain. How can these people be ruled who have this natural energy provided by nature? Rastas pay things mind that other people overlook; the small things that others don't care about, are the things we check.

RasTa Time

They can see what they can see and they have knowledge. So when they look at you, you look like a fool to them because they have knowledge of the true reality of life.

Rastas cannot hate. They realize that there is just a lack of knowledge, and they strive for that knowledge so that they can sit beside God.

We used to see these Rasta men, and little by little we started to communicate with them. They never begged us to communicate with them and they asked us for nothing. They would just pass us and go their own way. But people used to be afraid of them. If the Rastas saw something wrong happening, they would pass and say "Lightening, thunder and fire for that!" and then go on about their own business. So most people didn't like them. But there were some of us who wondered who these men were who just kept by themselves. We smiled at them and said, "Hey Dread" and they would respond with 'Ras Tafari.' Little by little, they would pass us and say 'so what did you learn at school today? Did you learn about Rastafari?' They never begged us to get to know them. We slowly forced ourselves in slowly, little by little, we learned more and more.

They never use words like how I am talking to you. They always used I & I. These are ancient words. Today we have the I-pad and the I-phone, but there was first the I.

We discovered what we had never learned before. We learned of a place named Ethiopia where there is a king who is the King of all the Kings of the world and is higher than all kings. Rastas never studied these things; they conceived it through the mystic.

KAS: What is the mystic? One of the songs Bob Marley sings is "Natural Mystic."

ACS: Yes. *"There's a natural mystic flowing through the air...if you listen carefully you will hear"*(*singing*). The Mystic is something that you can't hold nor see. It flows through the air, whistling the truth, and if you are searching in your mind and in your soul, you will pick it up. It is like a radio wave. But if you are not listening you cannot hear it.

If you are in school studying to be a lawyer or a doctor then you cannot pick up the *Mystic* because you are trying to learn something that somebody has written down. But the Rastas have another way of learning that is not written. It is knowledge that is blowing in the wind. It is from the heavens, and if you listen carefully, and follow the trail step by step, you will hear it and then the knowledge will come to you.

How could it be that when his Majesty Haile Selassie I visited Jamaica in 1966, everyone knew that their King was coming. It was never written in a book, but somehow all the people knew this was their King. How does that work? It was as if it were written in their hearts.

KAS: Did you get to see Haile Selassie?

ACS: I was little boy at that time, and that was my first journey to Kingston. My sister came to the countryside and took me to Kingston and that is how I saw His Imperial Majesty (HIM).

KAS: Can you recall what that visit was like?

When His Majesty came to Jamaica all you could see was a sea of faces. When this little man stepped off the plane thousands broke through the lines of police and soldiers and surged out onto the tarmac. He was given the biggest reception anyone ever received.

Caribbean News Weekly

His Majesty wore his hat down over his eyes. We used to say only bad boys wear their hat in that way. You couldn't see his face, and underneath he was watching everything.

The Rastafarians who had long revered HIM as Jah were present in full force. You could see it on the black & white TVs, everybody shouting "Jah! Ras Tafari!" The place went mad. The Rastas had come out of the hills from all around the island to greet HIM. There were hordes of them. Everyone was shocked to see how many of them there were, especially the government.

Everybody felt so good that His Majesty had come to Jamaica to bless us. Reporters asked him why He had come and He said that "he had wanted to see his people." So this is when we began to dig deeper and found that Ras Tafari is a deeper thing than we ever dreamed of. Everyone was Christian in Jamaica, but this is when the Rasta movement really began to spread.

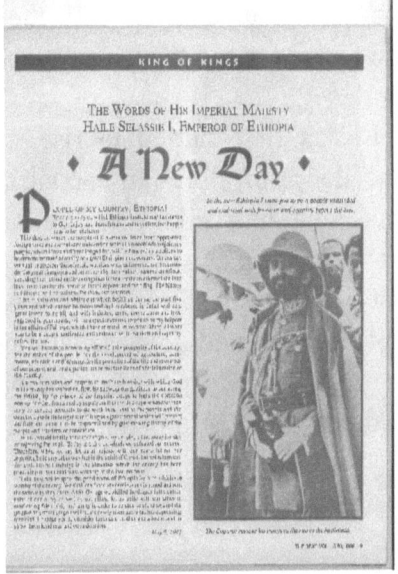

Beat Magazine Courtesy of Roger Steffens

KAS: Was Bob Marley there, too?

ACS: No. He wasn't there. Bob's mom had gotten a visa and had gone to America...

KAS: So Bob was not a Rasta before he left for America?

ACS: Yes, Rasta was in everybody's heart. But nobody could identify what it was. The Rastas were always communicating by themselves, but the government thought they were a cult and sent police and soldiers to run them away. Whenever they came down from the mountains to sell their organic produce, the forces chased them away.

When the Rastas first started to rise, there were signs on the doors of stores in Jamaica, "Wanted workers, but long hair piki piki need not apply. Don't want no niggah, no Ras Tafari." But when His Majesty was formally introduced to the Rastafarians He presented gold medallions to them. A group named Mystic Revelation played Nyabynghi drums for His Imperial Majesty.

RasTa Time

Caribbean National Weekly

At its root, Reggae music wasn't a thing to be sold. Reggae was a music that we believed we would play for HIM when we went back home to Ethiopia. The King gonna say to us, "you are in that place for so long, what did you learn?" And then we will start to play the Reggae music for HIM. That was the whole origination of Reggae. It wasn't about making money; we didn't have that intention. We thought we were going home. We thought we were going home. We had to move somehow and the music is the vehicle that takes us on the journey.

KAS: Bob Marley said to me that this was the generation that would see the truth. How can youth today see the truth?

ACS: If you want knowledge, you have to seek it, just like you study kanji or the ABC's or whatever script. You are born as a baby with a clear mind and you learn these things.

There is a meaning to all things, and there is a root to all things. What was hidden from the wise and prudent is now revealed to the babe and suckling. What was hidden from you before will be revealed because it is not a secret. God don't keep secret from people. Everything is going to be revealed little by little. The knowledge keeps increasing, and things that look impossible become possible.

KAS: Bob told me that one way to see the truth is through marijuana. He called it the herb, the healing of the nation….

ACS: I don't think a human being coming into the earth should make law, but the human came and made all kinds of laws, and then he make a law about a plant that was existing before he was here. That is ludicrous. People should never lash out against the herb because it give you a meditation and open up your heights that you can see the earth and yourself from a different level. Things that you never used to see on the earth, you see.

Everyone thinks Bob was such a big smoker, but when he was in the music, he did not remember anything—food, water or herb. He was just into the music.

KAS: What was Bob talking about when he sang "me belly full but me hungry?"

ACS: Everybody is born with a high spirit and you must find it. And how you find it? You have to listen. Bob is talking about love. He is talking about reality. What is reality? Your belly may be full, but sometimes you are still hungry, hungry for knowledge. You need something other than food. You need knowledge and the knowledge is in yourself. You just have to seek it. Nobody can force it down you.

When an angel like Bob Marley passes through on earth, you don't take his work lightly. I think we should give thanks and praise and listen and learn, because this is our time to dance. There is but just one dance, so you should dance good.

KAS: What do you remember of Bob Marley that brought that light in your life and that has sustained your belief in the Rasta movement?

ACS: He strengthen me and blow away the fears that kept me from growing in a spiritual way. Many people have fears—the skeleton in your closet. But there is a way that you can get rid of all that, and you have to find the way. Bob Marley found the way and he knew how to use it.

RasTa Time

My soul, my body, everything is a gift that is given to me. I am going to take care of that gift. Bob took his body and made that sacrifice for us. He didn't have to do 40 shows a month because he already had money. He could have gone and relaxed on some beach, but for your needs he want you to learn so he don't relax. He leave a tropical place to come to your world to tell you a message. So you should be grateful. He is not hungry for anything, he just come and give you a message…

Yes, man that is an angel.
And like I keep telling you that man have no time…
Man, when I think about it I really sorry for him. In such a short space of time he tried to do something.

KAS: But his message still lives on…….

ACS: First came Garvey who put out the word and then after he passed, Emperor Haile Selassie came. That meant there was something building up, and we still had so much to learn. We missed out of so many things through the hypocrisy of what goes on. Bob came to teach us but there is no time. So even if he was sick, he don't have time to search for physician. He have to be doing the work hoping that somehow he will get better by doing the work. He just hope and live in that hope.

There was no reason why Bob have cancer, especially that kind of cancer. I had a girlfriend whose father have that kind of cancer, and he called and called to all kinds of gods to come and kill him. But we played day and night with Bob and I never see he will feel bad, and then suddenly on one tour he have all the complaint and sickness that could kill a man. That man go and come, go and come until he die. How could Bob be so fit and then suddenly break down? And Bob was so fit. The only other thing that I see him do other than music is to keep physically fit and play soccer.

All Rastas are fit. People believed that the Rastas did not abide by the law and would attack us. So we had to defend ourselves. The first order we have is to make our bodies tough like a rock—climbing mountains, eating natural foods, and not junk food from the convenience store.

We walked so fast, that it was out of step with the ordinary people. When you walk faster than others, police shoot you because only robbers run….But Rastas walk fast because we are fit in both spirit and mind. Your breathing and pace is different from the ordinary people's life.

But Bob Marley whether he had cancer or candy or 'can this or can that'…he hear what other people would not hear. When the flesh had to wither away like a tree, he just accept it as life. It was the power of his job. He was on a mission and there was no time.

KAS: You used to help keep Bob fit by playing soccer with him.

ACS: Oh, come on, man, we were the working machine. We worked him for he cannot play alone. Bob and us played football every morning and every evening. We had no money and Bob had the ball. We were hungry but we had to play ball first and then he would give us food.

KAS: In a sense you kept him in shape for touring?

ACS: We did that but we didn't know we were doing that. He did marathon shows, and singing, dancing, and playing guitar require great concentration and being in good shape. I heard his woman say that wherever he went Bob would form a team. So, even when we were not there, anywhere he go he will gather some people, even take you off the street and say, 'come play some ball with me.'

Football is a rough thing and you cannot be so sick as Bob was and play that game. This is a man who worked 24/7 and just fall right down in his work. The one time he sick, he dead. He loved life. He wanted you to have life. This is a man who sacrificed his life for you to know the value of life. The work that he saw to do was such that his body cannot sustain it. It was all so fast......but his spirit is still here.

KAS: He told me that 'it is like I make a record in Jamaica and you listen to it and it make you feel good, but I don't have to be there."

ACS: There you go. There you go. (Laughs.)

He had already given up his life. He do forty something shows a month in the United States. You cannot do so much work as one man. You sing here and take a plane or a train and go sing there tomorrow. After you finish take a plane and a train. Come on, an elephant would die. (Laughs.) But he was trying to spread the message, as fast as his body could last. The work has to be done so he do it. That is the Mystic that is flowing inside Bob. But when you see it now, seeing is believing. In reality he was trying to spread soul.

RasTa Time

©*W. David Kubiak*

Kathy Arlyn Sokol

©*Michael Hofmann*

RasTa Time

On the Road

As Robert Burns says, 'the best laid schemes of mice and men often go astray'—and no matter how well organized you may think your plans are, it's always best to expect the unexpected. All that interview scheduling, hotel booking and ticket purchasing I had done ultimately had no bearing on the events that were about to happen over the next three months.

I flew out of Japan for Miami and Jamaica on the evening of March 10, had a long layover in Los Angeles, and by the time I woke up the next day in my Miami hotel, news of the devastating earthquake, tsunami and nuclear disaster in Japan was everywhere. Suddenly it all seemed unreal. What was I doing in Florida, chasing my dream of this book, when the country I had adopted as my home for some 30-odd years was suffering a major cataclysmic upheaval?

I couldn't reach anyone. I had no idea what was happening or how to proceed. I tried calling Ijichi Ryo, the project coordinator, and Factory A-Works, Ayumu's publishing company, to no avail. Phone lines were jammed or down and communication ultimately took days.

I had no choice but to continue my work on the book, since I had already scheduled a meeting the next morning with Antonio Godstone "Gilly Dread" Gilbert, who had been Bob's personal cook and assistant. Whether at home at 56 Hope Road in Kingston or on tour around the world, Gilly had always been at Bob's side, because Bob refused any food or drink that was not Ital, a Rasta word for food that is natural, pure and from the Earth. When traveling, Gilly would pack an old pirate-size trunk with roots, herbs and other natural ingredients from the homeland, and as they moved from city to city in their deluxe touring bus, Gilly would keep the King of Reggae refreshed with herbal teas and naturally blended juices.

Having adopted Rastafarianism as a young teenager, Gilly watched it evolve from an ostracized religion, whose Rastas were brutalized by police, army and god-fearing Christian citizens throughout Jamaica, to its now fashionable mystique; he and Bob would sit for hours reading the Bible, and 'reasoning', a practice similar to Judaic scholars debating the Talmud.

RasTa Time

Gilly and I talked for hours, and as he was leaving he turned to me and said that I was on a mission of great importance in bringing Bob's words and wisdom to the people; and he was here to help in any way. He said that it was RasTa Time that had taken me out of Japan right before the crisis, so that I could carry out my mission, and it was in Rasta Time that I would complete it.

Kathy Arlyn Sokol

Antonio Gladstone "Gilly Dread" Gilbert Interview

RasTa Time

KAS: Tell me a bit about your background and how you first met Bob Marley?

Antonio Godstone "Gilly Dread" Gilbert (GD): I was born in Kingston, Jamaica, and was just a regular local kid. I was a sports fanatic and played all kinds of sports — cricket, baseball, track and field, soccer, table tennis. I was a good soccer player and represented my country from the junior level, and Bob was a soccer enthusiast. He was six years older than me, and I looked up to him because of his music and what he stood for; and because I was a no nonsense soccer player he liked my mannerism for the game and was always supportive of me. It was amazing how we connected.

He had started in the Ska era, moved to rock steady, and then to reggae. He took reggae to the next level and it became the dominant music in Jamaica. My school was pretty close to where Bob had a record store in central Kingston. Kingston was the mecca of Reggae music, but a lot of the musicians like Bob came from Trenchtown. After school, I would ride my *lala* (bike) over there and hang out with them, you know, vibe with them.

Something drew me to the Wailers — Bob Marley, Peter Tosh and Bunny Wailer and I always kept track of them and knew where they were. I liked to be around them and their vibe. I listened to other groups, but there was something about them that caught my attention. They sang for the masses—the oppressed, the downtrodden, people that were being victimized and facing the struggles in Jamaica at that time.

RasTa Time

I had good relations with all the Wailers, but Bob had such charisma. His voice had me. He was like the point man, the real deal and I caught that right away.

KAS: *What songs especially touched you?*

GD: Wow, so many songs caught me. A very popular song in those days was *Simmer Down*. *Chicken merry, hawk de near and when him de near, you must beware, so Simmer down* Another one was *Rudie Let Him Go*.

(Sings)
Rudie come from jail 'cause rudie get bail
You frame him you say things he didn't do
You rebuke and you scorn, and you make him feel blue. You got to let him go...

KAS: *Was Bob part of the Rastafari movement then?*

GD: Yes, he was in natty dreads. In those days they classified us Rastas as rude boys because we were up against the "Babylonian system."

KAS: *How did Bob's early songs reflect the Rasta movement?*

GD: Rasta is about peace and love and togetherness. Self-reliance. That is what Bob took to the world through his music, teaching peace, love and goodwill amongst all people. In one of his songs he sings *"Give us the teachings of his Majesty, we don't want no devil philosophy."* His music was about oppression. And it was an oppression on Bob himself. It was not a bed of roses for him. I can tell you from my own experience as a young Rasta, life in Jamaica was bitter. Now you see all of these young Rastas in dreadlocks looking all relaxed and fine, but we paved the way for them.

The more I got into the Rasta movement, the more I understood self-reliance. A young Rasta in those days couldn't get a job. That is why I started cooking. Nowadays you see Rastas all over — in the banks, businesses, everywhere. All those people who used to put us down are now Rasta or trying to be a Rastafarian.

KAS: *What was it like to be a Rasta in those early days?*

GD: We communed together as brethren. All the Rasses, young and old, gathered at a place we called the House of Dreads. It was like a clubhouse where we played soccer and other sports. A section of the club had a lot of open space with bushes where we would chant and smoke and pray. Each of us had a small bible, and everyday we gathered together, and each person read a psalm or a passage from proverbs or the Songs of Solomon. We studied the Bible and knew it from Genesis to Revelation.

We would smoke the good herbs and chant and pray. For special occasions like the anniversary of the coronation of Haile Selassie I, we would have a big Nyah Binghi (drum) gathering with a bonfire in the middle. We would chant for seven days and seven nights, twenty- four seven. Non-stop. If you stopped playing the drum someone else would take over, and that drum kept beating for seven days, never stopping. The fire, too, was stoked for seven straight days as we all chanted and danced.

But whenever we would have a big celebration, the cops and the forces would come into our camp to intimidate I & I. It was like a war, only we didn't have any weapons. The only thing we had was our bible. We would just be praying and chanting, but they would attack us brutally. We had to be fit physically like a wild hare looking out for the forces to raid the camp because in those days smoking the herb was a mandatory jail sentence if you got caught.

I think that is why Jamaica is bleeding right now because we bled innocently. Imagine sitting with your bible, chanting, and the cops come with batons to bust your head open. We could have taken up arms and become like real gangsters because they were forcing us to become rebels. But all we wanted was to live with peace and love and show the world how to live in harmony.

So, all that you see happening in the world right now, we knew long ago that it was going to happen. That's what Bob sang about in his lyrics and it was his struggle to give this message around the world.

As a Ras you have to be true to the lifestyle and to the "livity." You can't be fake. And to help us make that transition into Rasta was the Wailing Wailers and their music. It was a mystical experience; a natural mystic for real for all the brethren I grew up with.

KAS: Part of your ceremonies included smoking marijuana. Bob called it the herb, the healing of the nation. What is its place in Rasta tradition?

GD: It is our sacrament. We use it to meditate and chant and commune together. It creates our communal vibe as we pray and chant for guidance and protection. Not for us, but for the whole universe. We never chant for I and I alone. We chant for the world to be a better place. But the forces don't want it to be like that; they want it to be a chaotic world.

KAS: How was the idea of His Majesty Emperor Haile Selassie as Rastafari first introduced in Jamaica?

GD: It was part of Marcus Garvey's philosophy. Garvey was a pioneer who brought the Back to Africa Movement to Jamaica in the 1920s. We grew up studying his philosophy, which focused on self-reliance and black consciousness, making people aware of their true identity. He talked of a black king from Africa who is the Black Messiah and was a catalyst for the Rastafari movement in Jamaica. The government didn't like what he was doing and eventually Garvey had to leave Jamaica, before we got our independence.

Time Magazine November 3, 1930

Many people became Rastafarian disciples in the 1920s and 30s and took up this movement despite the intense pressure from the government. Then when Haile Selassie I visited Jamaica in 1966, it was as if he waved a magic wand over us. More and more people became Rasta even though they were being beaten and victimized and terrorized and discriminated against for it.

I was just a teen and had been involved with my church, but I made the transition to Rastafarianism and my whole life changed. Because we chose our own identity, our own families turned against us. Rastas were the black sheep of their families and communities — the rude boys, the rebels. But when my generation came on board, we were more radical and we modernized the Rasta movement and took it to another level. The government couldn't understand how it had taken off so suddenly, and they got scared and considered us subversive.

KAS: So you were a soccer star but you were also a Rasta and had to learn self- reliance early on in your life?

GD: Yeah, I didn't get any help from my family. So, in order to survive I learned how to cook and hustle to earn money. Jamaican folks love to party and we would have dances every weekend. There were big dance halls and sound systems with the best music playing. I prepared all *Ital* food like potato and corn meal pudding and juices and sold it at the dance.

KAS: What is Ital food?

GD: *Ital* food is vegetarian food made without salt. We don't eat cheese, cow's milk or condensed milk, eggs, or any dairy products. We use a lot of beans in our cooking and all natural herbs. No packaged or bottled seasonings; only natural, fresh herbs. We try to eat properly and exercise a lot to stay healthy.

Rarely we eat fish. We also eat a lot of tofu. Actually we were the ones that popularized tofu in Jamaica. I remember in those days people put us down. They looked at the tofu and made a face and said why are you eating that garbage. But we were okay with it and now tofu is popular all over.

KAS: You became Bob's personal cook. What are some things that you prepared for Bob?

GD: Bob always liked his herb teas. Herb bush we call it. In Jamaica when we get up in the morning we drink a cup of fresh herb bush tea—natural herbs that grow wild, nothing off the shelf. You just walk outside and pick an herb and put it in boiling water. There are all different kinds of mints, sage, dandelion, search-me-heart, a wonderful tea that cleanses the heart, the body and the mind, and an herb we call fowl bone because the stalks look like chicken legs.

Every morning Bob would have his tea and then I would make some porridge—corn meal with plantain or banana, or oats with linseed and Irish moss (seaweed). I would always go on tour with a trunk like a pirate's chest full of herbs, honey, various roots, all this good stuff. I had everything in that huge trunk even pots and pans and my own utensils.

KAS: *I heard that Bob would never eat outside in a hotel or restaurants. He would only eat the food you prepared?*

GD: Sure right. Sometimes he would drink a bottle of natural juice. He was curious and wanted to taste the juices served in the different countries. But we stayed in the house to eat. During the day when we were on the road I made a lot of juices and protein shakes with wheat germ, almonds, cashews and spring water. For dinner, I would cook vegetables and make an Ital stew out of beans—red beans, broad beans, lima beans, black-eyed peas—and all different grains.

KAS: Can you share with us some recipes?

GD: I call this Gilly's 15-minute Tofu scramble. Use 1 or 2 packages of firm or medium-firm tofu and mash it with a fork. Heat some olive oil in an iron skillet and add the mashed tofu. Toss it for a few minutes until it is browned. Put in two stalks chopped celery and chopped bell pepper, diced red onion, and two cloves of minced garlic. Throw in some raisins, cranberries, raw cashews or other nuts, and then add a little thyme, rosemary, ½ teaspoon of turmeric or curry powder, some cayenne pepper and diced ginger. Last add diced plum tomatoes. Cook for a few minutes and then serve on top of brown rice or whole-wheat pasta or salad.

KAS: Did you make special food for Bob when you learned he had cancer?

GD: Bob didn't believe he had cancer. The doctors told him that the cancer would spread from his toe if they didn't amputate it. But his toe healed. He played soccer, jumped all over the place, doing what he does best. It was amazing how the sickness came over him. To this day I just can't believe that he died from cancer.

KAS: What do you think happened?

GD: It is unexplainable. There are some serious evil forces out there, you know. Bob Marley was too powerful for the world with his words and music, and I guess they didn't want the world to live in peace and love and togetherness. Each year it keeps getting more chaotic and I don't know when will it end.

KAS: In the interview that I did with Bob he said that 'it will all be over very soon,' that the world just could not keep on the way that we were living.

GD: Yeah, did you ever hear that song he sang One Love? *'One love is our weapon.'* And even now with what is happening in the world, love is still our weapon.

KAS: Two days before the 1976 Smile Jamaica Concert took place, there was an assassination attempt made on Bob, and both he and Rita Marley were shot. What happened?

RasTa Time

GD: It was a mad experience and totally wrong. It was a serious time. I was right there when they shot him up. It was election year, 1976, between Michael Manley's People's National Party (PNP) and Edward Seaga's Jamaica Labor Party (JLP). You know that song that Bob sings *"Never let a politician grant you a favor.... because they will always want to control you forever..."*

Bob was getting popular and recognized internationally, but Jamaican people were trying to keep him down and didn't give him the recognition that he deserved. In the 1970s when the whole world was looking at Bob, you couldn't even get the Jamaican radio stations to play his music. His music spread through the sound systems of the local dance halls, but for Bob to get air play at that time was a bitter experience. I don't even want to go into that. But eventually the radio station had to play his music because the people were calling for it and they wanted it. And Bob's words were being heard.

So, the same guys from the Babylon system who forced Marcus Garvey out of Jamaica came after Bob. They used our own people on that mission. People that Bob smoked with and shared good vibes with, turned around and sold out. Not to the highest bidder, but to what I would call the lowest bidder.

But despite being shot, two days later Bob went and did the concert as scheduled.

Bob had his work cut out for him, you know, he was on a mission. Nobody was going to stop his mission of bringing his music to the people and singing his words. He wasn't going to use any guns or bayonets or batons. He used his music to unite the people, and the government did not want the people to come together.

It was election year in 1976 and both political parties campaigned across the island. Manley sent his "emissary" to ask Bob to perform at the "Smile Jamaica" concert by his ruling party, PNP. There was a lot of tension leading up to the event, so Bob was given security detail. Every night the cops were at his house on Hope Road, but on the night of the shooting there were no cops. There was no protection. It was heavy stuff, I am telling you.

It was a Friday night when they came and shot up the place. Can you imagine? The guys were just playing music and rehearsing and then suddenly there were shots from all angles. We were defenseless. With the amount of shots that were fired it was a miracle how few people actually got hit. But through the powers of the Most High all our lives were spared.

It was pandemonium, chaos, and everybody ran for their lives. Rita got shot as she was leaving in her car to go home. I got out and kept on running. By the time the gunshots were over I heard the sirens. That is when the cops decided to come. I circled back and just then they were taking Bob and Rita up to the hospital. And I followed behind in one of the cars.

Beat Magazine Courtesy Roger Steffens

KAS: So the shooters just disappeared?

GD: Gone. But we knew where it was coming from. But Bob left it alone. He was the master, and he said to just let it roll, so we rolled with it. After the shooting, Bob didn't go back to Hope Road. He stayed at one of Chris Blackwell's properties up in the hills. It was like a hideout where he contemplated whether to do the show or get the hell out of Jamaica. But he did the show that Sunday and then flew out with Rita and the kids in a private jet before dawn the next day. Rita came back to Jamaica after things had calmed down in 1977. She told me that Bob wanted me to join them in London for the Exodus tour, so we flew off together.

Bob never wanted to go back to Jamaica. He was thinking of a movement toward Africa, the Movement of Jah People, Exodus. But after he had left, people in Jamaica were calling for peace, and the organizers of the One Love Peace Concert in 1978 asked Bob to come back and perform for the people.

KAS: The One Love Peace concert is famous for Bob bringing Prime Minister Michael Manley and opposition leader Edward Seaga onstage together to shake hands.

GD: Bob brought them up onstage to show the world that it is all about Peace and One Love. Even though he was not supportive of either party, Bob understood the ideals of socialism. Michael Manley was a big supporter of Castro because of his humanitarian causes. Cuba came to Jamaica's aid several times and provided us with medical teams, programs for training doctors, construction works...you name it. Manley was all about socialism, he didn't want to go communist, but the political forces figured Manley was taking Jamaica toward the left. Manley was preaching to the Jamaican folks about self-reliance and developing our own resources, and we didn't need any outside agencies like the IMF, which had completely destroyed our domestic infrastructure and our economy. It was all about the destabilization of Jamaica.

KAS: This was all happening in Jamaica at the same time that the Rasta movement was growing in the 70s?

GD: Yes, even Prime Minister Manley visited Ethiopia to meet Emperor Haile Selassie I. He came back to Jamaica with what he called the *Rod of Correction* and said that the Emperor had given it to him. Manley took the moniker Joshua. Then

Manley used the Rasta vibe as a ploy to help him in his election campaign. Because the Wailing Wailers lived in Manley's constituency in Trenchtown, and because of their popularity and their identity with the people, Manley asked them to join his all-island campaign tour in 1972.

KAS: Can you talk a bit about 1979 and what you remember of Bob's Japan tour? It must have been quite different from the other places that you had visited.

GD: Yes, you are right. Japan was such a disciplined country with its deep principles and traditional culture. It was very different from Jamaica and other countries we traveled to. So for the promoters to have Bob and the Wailers in Japan at that time was an honor. Overwhelming. You were there; you saw the response from the folks. I mean, every concert was sold out.

KAS: Yeah, I was there.

GD: Remember, we stayed at the Sun Route Hotel and the Osaka Grand Hotel. We went to Tokyo, Osaka, and Kyoto and rode that Bullet train. (laughs) Wow, it is good to know you were there.

RasTa Time

The love that we got from the people was so beautiful. It was an awesome experience.

Courtesy of Hideki Nakagawa

In Japan, we were fortunate to be able to use the kitchen facilities at the hotels where we stayed. Normally Bob would book a suite so that I could cook right there. But in Japan, the hotels gave me a section in their kitchen to cook and even gave me brand new utensils to use. The Japanese chefs were really curious about my cooking and would gather around me to taste my dishes and learn my style of cooking. And I learned a lot from them too. It was a very moving experience for me.

When we left Japan, Bob was talking about going back.

KAS: *Did you get to play any soccer in Japan?*

GD: Yeah, we played soccer in every country we went to. Bob was such an ardent soccer player and enthusiast that we always traveled with our soccer balls on the road. We would even play in the hotel rooms. We would move all the furniture and if we broke anything, Bob would pay for it.

In each country, the promoters always arranged a soccer game with local clubs. This demonstrated what Bob stood for—natural eating, good health, exercise.

KAS: *What other tours stand out in your mind?*

GD: One of the most memorable times was when Bob was invited by the government of Zimbabwe to become part of the commemorative independence day event. Rhodesia was becoming Zimbabwe, and apartheid was coming to an end. Bob's music was like an anthem for the people of Zimbabwe.

RasTa Time

(singing)
Every man gotta right to decide his own destiny,
And in this judgment there is no partiality.
So arm in arms, with arms, we'll fight this little struggle, 'Cause that's the only way we can overcome our little trouble.

Courtesy Jack Low

When we got off the plane in Zimbabwe, it was overwhelming to see the reception they gave him. They rolled out the red carpet, and the first ones to meet us were Robert Mugabe, the new president of Zimbabwe, and his cabinet ministers in a single file.

They shook each of our hands and said, "Welcome Home!" It was a powerfully moving moment for me and for all of us.

KAS: What did you personally get from your relationship with Bob? What do you hold in your heart everyday when you think of this man?

GD: What I liked about Bob was his commitment, his discipline, his principles and what he stood for in life. He had a beautiful charisma and a beautiful soul. He was a good giver and just wanted to see the world be a better place. Yeah, I am all for that, and I will always support him. I lift my hat to him. I mean, if he was going to war I would go to war with him. He gave me a life, a beautiful life. It is unexplainable. He was a special angel, and more than a prophet in his time.

You can see what is happening with his music now. It is all over the world. His music is the manifestation of his life, of the work he came here to do. His kids continue with what he fought for and stood for. He wanted to see all nations come together. All colors, class, creed. It was overwhelming to see the power that Bob had around the world and how people everywhere embraced his music. His teachings were conveyed through his music. He was gathering the people and bringing them together from all over the world. And the powers that be didn't want that.

Bob Marley music is message music. He may have been in the music entertainment world, but at the same time he was getting his message across. Life, happiness, love. Sensual. He covered all angles. He covered the triangle. The best thing that happened to me in life is meeting Bob Marley and the Wailing Wailers. Bob Marley was like a god to me.

Rastafari, Haile Selassie I, the First Lives and Reigns Forever and Ever. Jah bless. Peace and Love for a better world.

RasTa Time

©*Faith Kubiak*

Ky-Mani

My first challenge was to find a way to meet the Marley family. Four of the Marley brothers—Ky-Mani, Stephen, Damian and Julian—were the featured acts in the Nine Mile High Festival, one of many commemorative events marking the 30th year of their father's passing. The Festival was taking place on March 12, my second day in Miami, just across the street from my hotel in Bayfront Park.

I headed over to the venue in the hope of meeting one of the Marley boys, but with particular interest in getting an interview with Ky-Mani, who had recently published a controversial book called *"Dear Dad."*

The son of Bob and Anita Belnavis, a table tennis champion in Jamaica, Ky-Mani had not grown up in the wealth of his siblings. Instead, he'd been raised in a Miami ghetto and was on the fast track to becoming a gangster when he'd turned to music and acting. Considered the "bad boy" of the clan, I thought he might have some interesting perspectives on the growing Marley dynasty.

While waiting for Ky-Mani to appear at his tent, where he was to sign autographs and T-shirts, I hung out with the designer Homer Bair, an older Rasta who had started the *Cooyah (look here!)* brand of clothing, and now, through his *CY (see why?)* line, is creating t-shirts for Ky-Mani. When Ky-Mani arrived at the tent, Homer introduced us. I quickly briefed Ky-Mani on the rediscovered "lost" interview and my time with his father. He listened respectfully, promised an interview and gave me a couple of telephone numbers where I could reach him.

The Continental Bayside

Before the massive crowd began mobbing out of the performance venue, I slipped away and returned to my hotel. The Continental Bayside Hotel provides little in the way of amenities but is big on making people feel at home. Since it is run by a group of mostly Cuban exiles, Spanish is the predominant language spoken by staff and guests alike.

When I first arrived, an elderly man of about seventy-five and barely five feet tall assisted me with my bags. He looked too frail to even lift the suitcase onto the bell cart. Once we got into the elevator, he asked where I was from. When I told him I was from Japan, he suddenly put his shoulders back and told me that he had studied aikido and karate since he was a boy. To prove it, he flexed his arm muscles, showing that his earlier heavy-lifting antics were for theatrics only. Half Cuban, half Chinese, he had also practiced Asian healing arts like *reiki*. He had the late night shift, and every night I would be in the lobby working on the Internet and trying to reach Japan. He and I would often talk, and when I was exhausted by the day's events he would give me *reiki* treatments, right in the middle of the lobby.

The days drifted by as I waited for confirmation from Ky-Mani about the interview. The call never came. Frustrated, I decided to get out of the hotel and go to Bayfront Park, to sit and meditate where the Marley had played. There I closed my eyes, and as if he were standing in front of me, Bob Marley's face appeared. He simply said, "everyt'ing in time, mon; everyt'ing in time."

I was now getting to "overstand" Rasta Time. Overstand is a Rasta word meaning "the state of mind that emerges when all illusions are removed; the idea that one should not 'understand' or 'stand under' an idea but overstand it—absorb and correctly perceive it."

When Gilly said he would, 'come soon,' it did not mean that he would come at any appointed time; he would come when the experience of the moment indicated the 'right time,' RasTa Time. And it was with a steady rhythm in RasTa Time that Gilly guided me through the streets of Miami and into the Rasta world of Bob Marley's friends and family.

STEPHEN MARLEY

Gilly had arranged for me to meet Stephen Marley one night at Stephen's studio, where he was rehearsing for his upcoming '*Roots of Life Tour*'. As we drove to the studio, Gilly put Bob Marley's final concert performance into the CD deck and turned the volume all the way up. *Bob Marley and the Wailers Live Forever* recorded live on September 23, 1980, at the Stanley Theater in Pittsburgh, Pennsylvania, filled the car and wrapped us in its power. It had been recorded only two days after Bob had collapsed while jogging in Central Park, when in New York to perform before a sell-out crowd of over 20,000 at Madison Square Garden. The cancer that he had been diagnosed with three years earlier had spread, and he was told to stop touring. When the promoter of the Pittsburgh show, Rich Engler, asked Bob if he could still perform, he reportedly replied, "Mon, I wasn't going to, but I'm going to now, for my band and everybody. It's a sold-out show. I'm going to do it." [1]

As Gilly and I sang along with the King of Reggae, he reminisced about the power of that final appearance; it had been as if Bob had known that there would be no more. I recalled those magical nights on tour with Bob in April 1979, dancing not in the side aisle, but on the side of the stage, where no usher could force me to sit down; and how sometimes Bob would look in my direction, just near the curtain, as if testing the pulse of his backstage retinue, to check if I was dancing.

Now, as I sat in this car, as Bob's voice came pouring into the air from the speakers right beside my head singing *Running Away*.

I paused to give thanks for the amazing circumstances and coincidences that had brought me to this moment with Bob Marley's personal assistant, who was taking me to listen to Stephen Marley up close and personal, in his rehearsal studio.

---

[1] *http://www.post-gazette.com/pg/10266/1089451-388.stm?cmpid=newspanel0*

At about 10pm, Gilly turned into a warehouse lot in the upscale area of Kendall on the outskirts of Miami. When he got out of the car, a ring of Rastas — including Stephen's eldest son, Joseph, and his nephew (Bob Marley's grandson) Matthew — surrounded and greeted him. We opened the warehouse door to a sea of faces of all ages inside, from a newborn nursing in its mother's arms to the older Rastas who had come to see how the next generation was carrying the rhythms of Reggae forward. Photos and posters of Bob Marley were everywhere, even in the toilet. I was tempted to take some photos but felt as if it would be an intrusion.

Stephen was in full rehearsal mode, sitting on a stool in the center of his band, which was composed of two keyboard players, two drummers, two female backup vocalists, guitar, bass, flute and sax. I took a seat on the edge of the couch, reminding myself that this was not a concert but a rehearsal and that these folks were here to work, so I literally kept to the edge of my seat and refrained from dancing. The mood suddenly shifted as Stephen started strumming on his guitar and gently intoned *Now I Know*, a song from his newest album, *The Revelation Part 1: the Root of Life*.

RasTa Time

Tears began flowing from my eyes as I listened to its passionate phrasing, its intimate insight into the fleeting nature of life; I felt even greater respect and love for Bob Marley, who had fathered such a creative and caring soul.

Stephen Robert Nesta Marley is the second son of Bob and Alpharita (Rita) Constantina Anderson, who were married in a simple ceremony in Trench Town in 1966. Stephen was born on April 20, 1972, in Wilmington, Delaware, where Rita had joined her mother-in-law, Cedella Booker, while Bob was focusing on his first album, *Catch a Fire*, for Island Records' founder, Chris Blackwell.

Stephen has acted mainly in the role of producer in the family, with one of his earliest successes the innovative 1999 remix disc *Chant Down Babylon*, which paired recordings of his father with such hip-hop stars as Lauryn Hill and Eryakah Badu. It also featured Damian, Julian and Stephen himself, a concept that he expanded upon when he invited Ziggy and Ky-Mani to join the brothers for a 27-city *Bob Marley Roots, Rock, Reggae Festival tour* that he produced in 2004, and that marked their first official performance together onstage. Back in 2005, Stephen produced *Welcome to Jamrock* for Damian, which won two Grammy awards, including

Reggae Album of the Year, and has become one of the most watched Rasta YouTube videos ever, with over 160 million hits.

Although Stephen had sung backup with his siblings Ziggy, Cedella and Sharon since the age of 8 as part of *Ziggy Marley and the Melody Makers,* a group formed in 1979 when Bob wrote *Children Playing in the Streets* for them to record, he did not release his own solo album until 2007 (*Mind Control)*. He wanted it to be just right, and says of his music, "The only sense of obligation I have when I create music is that it has to have integrity…Content is what gives music integrity….there is no content in the commercial side of music. That is what I am here to correct."

Stephen is a true family man, sharing his Jamaican and Miami homes with his tribe of 13 children. With his brother Ziggy he also founded Ghetto Youth in 1993, to help underprivileged kids in Jamaica learn basic skills and participate in building their community. Ghetto Youths International, the Marley brothers record label imprint, promotes fresh young talent like Chris Ellis, son of famed Jamaican singer Alton Ellis, who back in the 60s was crowned the Godfather of *Rock Steady*. Of course Stephen brings his own kids on tour with him, just like Bob brought him along on his tours; the two nights Gilly brought me to the rehearsal, Stephen's 21-year-old son Joseph took center stage, adding hip-hop jive to the reggae mix.

Stephen's third self-produced album *"Revelation Part 1: The Root of Life"* was conceived as a celebration of and way of preserving his father's style of roots rock reggae. "My father used to tell us," he once recalled, "music is like a prayer and you don't put just anything in a prayer, you say important things, pray for people who are suffering. He'd say don't take it for a joke and if you're not really serious don't do it." [2]

Stephen has taken it seriously and believes that the messages in his father's music and in his own music need to be heard again and again. "Reggae's consciousness," he says, "was built on a message, a Black movement, Rastafari, and that is not being pushed today. Me know me have power with my voice and my instrument, so, with that vibe, me picked up me guitar, strummed a reggae rhythm, and just started singing; from song to song, that is the spirit within this album."

---

[2] *http://www.amazon.com/Revelation-Part-1-Roots-Life/dp/B004L36M5Y*

Although I and my mission had been introduced to Stephen, in the world of the Rasta one does not just come up and say, "It's nice to meet you. Can I interview you now?" First one must "vibe," just hang out, be a natural part of the scene. When the second rehearsal session ended, as Gilly drove me to Stephen's house, he nonchalantly informed me that Stephen would be leaving in a couple hours to go on tour.

When we got to the house, the place was abuzz with people packing up and loading the van, in preparation for a dawn departure. I surveyed the hectic scene around me and concluded that the chances for an interview were slim. But knowing that this was my only opportunity, at 2am I gingerly approached Stephen as he sat at his computer and asked if he would like to hear an excerpt of the interview I'd done with his father. He nodded and soon we were sitting on the couch together in the midst of all of the chaos as Stephen listened intently to his father's words. He then turned to me and said that he would be happy to share a few thoughts with me.

RasTa Time

Afterward, I stared in disbelief at the recorder still in my hand that had just captured some moments with Stephen Marley. I reflected on where I was, whom I was with, and the music and the message that had carried me there. It seemed I had found a place where I belong.

Kathy Arlyn Sokol

STEPHEN MARLEY
INTERVIEW

RasTa Time

***KAS:** In the interview that I did with your father back in 1979 in Japan, he said, "it is the Truth that keeps it going and to know that you are doing it for a purpose..."and that "this is the generation that will see the light." Today as the son of Bob Marley, the next generation, how are you moving his message forward?*

SM: Carrying the light of God, the light of enlightenment, the light of truth, the light of equality, the light of love, the light of justice. That is the light we are carrying through our music.

Music is our source, our medium, and our way of bridging the gap. I know no other way of expressing myself than through my guitar and my voice and the gift that God gave me — the ability to put words together that make you feel good. It is like medicine going down with a bit of sugar. But that is how I share the light.

We also get our message across through our beings, through ourselves. Anyone that we come across in our lives, even separate from the music we make, we influence by the way that we live. You said that you met my father, and just by meeting him, he didn't sing to you, but by meeting him, just him, just Bob, it changed you and your life.

So we get the message out through our music and our lives. We are living testimonies. We are not perfect. But we try.

KAS: You told me that you are connected to your father through spirit.

SM: It is not just about DNA, and not just about being the son of a man. It is more than that. Because there are a lot of fathers and sons out there who are separate in their purpose and their outlook on life. Right? For me and my father, and I can say for my entire family, we are bonded more spiritually and look at things more from the spiritual side. We have the same passion and we serve God to the fullest, and within all of that we have this connection to each other that goes beyond blood. It has to do with spirit.

KAS: You were born as a Rasta. What does that mean to you?

RasTa Time

SM: Rasta is God; the manifestation of God. He manifests Himself different to you than He manifests himself to me. Rasta is the Truth, but it is I & I Truth that He reveals only to I & I. You see, the main thing is that there is one God. There is only one God even if you call him Daddy. All Him can tell you is the Truth. I cannot impose my belief on others, but it is the Truth. Yet it is not to be imposing. It just is.

KAS: As we sit here in the middle of the night, you are preparing to set out for another month of touring. What keeps you going night after night?

SM: God and Man. God and Man. God will always be the forefront. There is so much things I can say. I must always come back to God first because he is the Light. It is not like God have some magnificent speech. No, it is very simple. See God first. It is simple. It is not Pythagoras. It is plain. Even a baby can understand it.

KAS: Tonight in your rehearsal you sang one of your new releases called 'Now I Know.' What do you now know?

SM: *'Now I Know'* is a song about realization. But everyone takes from each of my songs what they need; no matter what my inspiration was in writing it. I could have been talking about anything. It is the person listening who interprets it for themself. I could have been writing about something very insignificant but even if my inspiration was a small, petty thing, when it transcends to the world and the cosmic powers of the world it does what it needs to do. That is the power of music.

KAS: You also sang some of your father's songs tonight. Are there any particular songs of his that you like to sing?

SM: All of them.

You speak of our father. He is our father, but he was more than that to us all also. And that is the special part of it. I was his son, but what Bob means to me is much more than just being my father because you have biological fathers that don't really "father" their children. But Bob was our mentor, our skipper, our captain.

Bob is instilled in me. So, when I sing my father's music, I don't really think, "Oh, I am going to sing a Bob song." His music is a part of me. So, it doesn't come out like that, it comes out of me just as a natural thing like the birth, and the earth and the root and the tree. Like him say, "you can't bend an old tree might as well chop it down, but if it is a young tree, you can steer the young tree." He steered us. I want people to know that. He was not just our father, and we are not following in the footsteps of our father because he was our father. He was much more than that. He was our mentor, our teacher, our skipper, so it is much deeper than just being his son.

KAS: Bob's song 'One Love' has become an anthem around the world? What does that song mean to you?

SM: The message is always the same message. We cannot recreate the message because it is the Truth; and there is only one Truth. We have to speak it. We don't care who say it. It just so happens that it was my dad. Sometimes people ask what is the message. It is all about 'One Love.' Life have different pages and stages, but if you really have to sum it up it, it is that song. It is a song of Oneness. We are equal. No matter what, we are the same. One Love gave that message. It said it all.

You could go up to a person you don't even know, a total stranger, and say, "One love, my brother. One love, my sister." And they would know what you are saying. That song is a message of togetherness, without laying down a sermon for people for two hours and then everyone leaves.

It is a good message to carry with you always.

RasTa Time

Kathy Arlyn Sokol

KING SPORTY

Interviewing King Sporty, the man who originally penned *Buffalo Soldier*, was a different kind of challenge. Having been one of the most popular deejays in Jamaica, the King was not about to lend his voice to the project until he better understood the object of my mission.

The first time Gilly brought me to King Sporty's house, just a few miles north of my hotel on Biscayne in downtown Miami, we found the King in his backyard, creating an *ikebana* flower arrangement. On either side of the walkway that led to his house, he had designed a vibrant garden, with flowering plants and fruiting trees, many of which were original to Jamaica, like mango and breadfruit. Keeping to a strict Rasta diet, the King also grew herbs and roots, like thyme and scallion, to season his Ital dishes.

A slight gentleman, just five feet tall and weighing about 50 kilos, King Sporty's bearing is regal, reflecting his early years of karate training. It was hard to believe that this man was born in 1943 and had fathered 24 children; he looked closer to 40 than nearly 70, and his voice was as melodious as it was when he first began his musical career.

RasTa Time

Few people know his real name (Noel Williams) or his enduring role in musical history. Recognized by the International Reggae & World Music Hall of Fame with a Lifetime Achievement Award, Noel Williams has been recording and releasing music on his own *Konduko* and *Tashamaba* labels for over 30 years. Married to Betty "Queen of the Miami Sound," Wright, who opened for Bob Marley on the *Survival Tour*, music surrounds his everyday life.

Courtesy King Sporty

Kathy Arlyn Sokol

Born in the small Jamaican town of Port Antonio, Noel became a Rasta in his early teens, often taking part in the seven-day, seven-night Nyah Binghi (drumming) festivals at which the Rastas gathered to pray, chant and drum. The police regularly raided these gatherings and brutalized the Rastas. The 15-year-old Noel sought a less confrontational road to Rasta consciousness and discovered his path in words. He began deejaying while still in high school and went on to become one of Jamaica's earliest dub poets, adopting the name King Sporty.

At a time when Jamaican radio banned reggae music and many deejay 'dub poets', people streamed to the "sound systems," large mobile discos with giant speakers set up in ball parks or ballrooms, to dance to the latest hits. Deejays like King Sporty kept the crowds grooving to the music with improvised sarcastic wit and dub lyricism. Deejaying in those days was a form of creative rebellion; King Sporty found his freedom and a voice in music, inspiring jive and poetic teaching.

RasTa Time

Watch the change
And see how it remains the same
Change the music
But it remains the same
Can't find a new note
Different corners
To take different curves...
                               King Sporty

He settled in Miami in 1963, and took his one-man band, King Sporty & the Invisible Man to sea, performing in cruise ship nightclubs. One night aboard ship, an elderly white engineer told him the story of the Buffalo Soldiers; the King then began to research their history. Inspired by them, he wanted people to know who these men were and what they'd stood for; out poured the lyrics of Buffalo Soldier.

"Buffalo Soldier," King Sporty surmises, was the name Native Americans gave to the black slaves arriving from Africa, partly because their hair resembled the mane of a bull buffalo, but mostly because of their fierce fighting spirit. The Indians, the King continued, also revered the buffalo because it provided everything that made their life possible...food, clothing and shelter.

It was not long before black soldiers themselves embraced the name. When America's Civil War broke out in 1861, roughly 200,000 Blacks enlisted in the Union Army, which promised them an end to slavery. Although slavery was abolished at the war's end, racial segregation continued, even in the Army. The U.S. Congress, however, did recognize the Black soldiers' remarkable valor, and established the first all-black cavalry regiments. The black 10th Cavalry, formed in Kansas in 1886, featured the buffalo in its coat of arms, and soon the Native Americans' admiring label became synonymous with all the African-American regiments.

As a song, *Buffalo Soldier*, has become one of Bob Marley's most iconic anthems. Like many Rastas,

RasTa Time

Marley identified with the Buffalo Soldier's history and it fired his imagination. Although Bob recorded the song in 1980, it was only released posthumously with his version first appearing on the 1983 *Confrontation* album, which became a #4 hit in the United Kingdom. The song's popularity continues to soar.

In October 2010, when the last of the Chilean miners emerged from their 2-month ordeal trapped 2000 feet underground, among one miner's first requests was to hear *Buffalo Soldier*, which the men had sung to keep their spirits strong. King Sporty rewarded them with a brand new version.

He is now developing another history-based tribute song, *Ordinary Soldier,* dedicated to the legendary Tuskegee Airmen and the all-black 555th paratrooper battalion, the Buffalo Soldiers of the sky during World War II.

One of the King's last releases, *Signs of the Time*, included his newest version of the song.

*King Sporty died on January 5, 2015

Courtesy King Sporty

KING SPORTY
INTERVIEW

Kathy Arlyn Sokol

KAS: Known as one of his most iconic anthems, how is Buffalo Soldier emblematic of Bob Marley's message?

King Sporty: (singing)
Said he was a Buffalo Soldier, win the war for America....
Buffalo Soldier, Dreadlocked Rasta....
....We fought on arrival
and we are still fighting for survival.

As long as man continue to live and hurt we will always be fighting for survival. When we arrived we were fighting and throughout our lives we are still fighting.

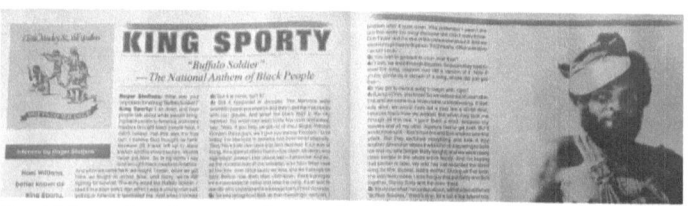

Beat Magazine Courtesy Roger Steffens

That song was written out of the inspiration of the desperation of the early days when people didn't understand what was right and wrong. Who is right? Who is wrong? One man's hero is the other man's terror. Who knows if you should go up or down?

RasTa Time

These things are life's mystery. Not all has been told or written. We have to figure these things out for ourselves. If we live along with the lifestyle of humanity and be humble and treat each other right and spread love…..that is what Bob Marley was all about.

When I wrote *Buffalo Soldier* and performed it several times, people liked the song. When Bob heard it, he said, "Hey man, that is my song." And he was my favorite messenger. We grew up together from little boys—Bob, Peter, Bunny. All of us was at Studio One.

My name is Noel Williams, but my friends and well-wishers call me King Sporty. I started my musical career on the west side of Kingston, Jamaica. My brother-in-law, they called him Count C the Wizard, had a sound system and we used to be dancing around the box day and night, and talking trash. And one night at a nightclub, he throwed me the mike and said, "Go for yourself." And this is where I am at today. From being a dub poet in Jamaica, to a rapper, a singer, a performer, overall entertainer, producer and a writer. Most of all, I am a messenger.

And God has blessed me with these things because of my association with real people like Bob Marley in the music industry. I started out as a mechanic as my occupation. And my occupation has taken me to a wonderful situation, and I still have not found my destination.

Valzarok Creative Commons Wikipedia

But most of the people who do music, who are poets, preachers, teachers….that is how I looked at Bob Marley. He was a poet, he was a human being who even in talking to you, without music, there was this resounding vibration of life.

And I might be one of the only persons, or maybe a few other guys who thought like me, who didn't believe that Bob died too young. We believed that he did so much, and when God got ready, He took him. A lot of us here are carrying on the work that he left behind. We are still writing songs and still making music. And when all the devastation is over, we will ask Gabriel to blow his horn and let the people rejoice again.

So when we are sitting here talking about the histories and the different things that happen in life, we are supposed to be prepared. My heart goes out for the people in Japan and the earthquake and nuclear disaster they experienced. Japan is not the only place that went through devastation, but some places get hit more than others. I am here in America and 350 people died in Mississippi, Alabama and Tennessee or maybe more from tornado.

These are the elements of God, not of man, and what God does to His creation, to me is not really destruction. It is reconstruction. 'Cause after the earthquake, when you go back to a place, it was reconstructed. Some people might call it devastation. But from the Almighty's side it is a form of reconstruction.

Devastation exists around the universe. It is not just located in certain geographical locations.

Devastation is a phenomenon where man is worried and scared to understand what is really happening in this life that we are living.

KAS: How does Buffalo Soldier relay that understanding?

KS: It is the message. The awakening. And when I told Bob how I got the story....it was like....I was working on the ship at the time, and an old white man, an engineer was telling us about different things, and he asked me as a Jamaican, because I was dreadlocks at the time and most of the guys on the ship were scared of me, and he said to me, "Man, there were some guys who used to look like you. They were called the Buffalo Soldiers."

That is how I first found out about the Buffalo Soldiers. Three hundred miles out in the middle of the ocean, sailing a tugboat, called Rescue. We used to pick up ships that were stranded at sea. I was the youngest man ever to work on that boat. So maybe I was placed on that boat to learn some stuff that was hidden from us. And as a Jamaican I was really excited, so I read the book. The song was just three minutes of a book that took me five hours to read. And the message went across.

RasTa Time

If you know your history
Then you should know where I'm coming from
Then you wouldn't have to ask me who I think I am....

When the Native Americans first glimpsed the black men arriving in ships from Africa, they saw their fighting spirit, and feared them and bowed down to them, and called them the Buffalo Soldiers. The buffalo provided the Indians with all the basic necessities like food, clothing, and shelter; and symbolized everything that made things work for them. (Chanting):

The Buffalo Soldier
The dreadlocked Rasta,
Helped and won the war for America.
We were taken from the mainland and sent to the Caribbean…..

And that is how we wound up in Jamaica. We went way beyond, and this is the whole idea of the song. It is in reference to what is, what was, and what is still going on. The Buffalo Soldiers figured out how to survive, just as the Dreadlock Rastas did.

Kathy Arlyn Sokol

Everyday is a mystery and everyday people are still fighting for survival. It will never end on this planet, so we better try to make things right. But do we really know what is right and what is wrong? Not all has been told or written. We have to figure these things out for ourselves.

When one of the guys who was trapped in a mine in Chile, came out from 2000 feet underneath the bottom of the pit of the earth to the surface, they asked him, "What would you like us to do for you?" And he said, "I would like to hear Bob Marley's *Buffalo Soldier*."

I sat in my room and I felt inspired to know that I had something to do with this song and that I had a real messenger to spread those words around the world.

God bless Bob Marley and all his family. As long as I live I will always remember this man as a very close brethren. One love.

RasTa Time

Courtesy King Sporty Family

Kathy Arlyn Sokol

MONTEGO BAY & RASTA COMMUNITY

With Ky-Mani still difficult to pin down for an interview, I moved on to Montego Bay in Jamaica, where I waited for Gilly to come from Miami and guide me across the island to Kingston. I found myself at one of those massive, gated hotels, where a stay comes with all-you-can-eat buffets and free drinks. Once you have checked in, there is little to do but drink, eat and be merry. Jamaican dancing classes are held poolside, along with modified versions of games like Musical Chairs, while volleyball is offered on the beach just meters from the famous crystal waters of Montego Bay.

RasTa Time

I spent a few hours one day engaging in the play but couldn't shrug off the uneasy sense of manufactured mirth and merriment. I was in Jamaica and wanted to spend my time with Jamaicans, not a bunch of people who had come on a deluxe-three-day package tour. Just outside the gates, however, a few meters beyond the pier that demarcates the hotel's boundary, there was a community of Rastas.

A sign warns hotel patrons to leave the premises at their own risk. I ventured out, and within a few feet of entering the community, was befriended by Patrick, a young Rasta, who cheerfully escorted me into the Jamaica I had been seeking.

The Rastas had set up shops selling handcrafted masks, jewelry and souvenir items fashioned in makeshift outdoor studios under fruiting almond trees. The small boats with which they fished in the stillness of the night and returned with the dawn were beached along the shore.

RasTa Time

After visiting the Rastas for a couple of days, I played my interview of Bob Marley for them, feeling somewhat shy, knowing that these people were living Bob's words, while I had just been their lucky recipient. Of some who had gathered around to listen to the interview, I asked their response.

My friend Patrick said that a Rasta was someone strong enough and courageous enough to live in the mystic. Bob Marley, he continued, showed the world the dignity and indomitable spirit of the Rastaman.

RasTa Time

Angela, a middle-aged black woman born in Jamaica but raised in London, told me that she had always been a Rasta, and had come back to Jamaica to be part of a true community. "Being a Rasta, representing peace and love to all, regardless of who you are, cannot be a bad thing. We need the One Love Bob talks about in our collective lives. As Bob foretold, we have to stand firm, stand strong as the world around us faces countless struggles.

Rasta Charlie believes, "Bob is still the greatest, still number one, and even though he is dead, he is a legend and his music still teach."

Cool Donavan simply said that "Bob was the man who make people take reggae music serious – and to understand its Rasta roots."

RasTa Time

Returning to the resort and the endless and tiresome games organized to keep its guests amused; I turned my gaze one last time toward Patrick and my other new friends. They had walked with me to the pier, but stopped as we approached the walkway, a simple plank of wood set in the sand, that was to them a warning to go no further. I bowed deeply, grateful for their genuine mirth and merriment.

Kathy Arlyn Sokol

RasTa Time

KINGSTON

Back in my hotel room, I prepared for Gilly's planned noon arrival. At 11am I received a call letting me know that he had made it to the Miami airport on time, but had forgotten his passport, and that he would 'soon come'.

The plan had been for him to join me in Montego Bay and drive through the countryside to Kingston, where I had an appointment the next morning with the Honorable Edward Seaga, the man who Bob Marley had brought on stage with Michael Manley at the One Love Peace Concert in 1978, and who had become the Prime Minister of Jamaica for nearly 10 years.

Arranging the interview with the former Prime Minister had taken months, and Gilly had forgotten his passport! I anxiously considered other forms of transportation to Kingston, but then decided to simply trust that everything would work out all right and spent the day downloading the photos and interviews I had taken of the Rastas.

RasTa Time

Gilly arrived at about 10pm and we started out on the winding, poorly lit, potholed, four-hour drive to Kingston. People at the hotel had admonished us not to leave so late at night, since Gilly had not been back in Jamaica for 12 years and the road had changed. But Gilly is a warrior, and in the pre-dawn hours – the period called the "second watch" in Buddhist lore, when Shakyamuni is said to have attained enlightenment – we entered the city limits.

Rather than checking into a hotel, Gilly brought me to his son Mark's house in Drew's Land, once an upscale neighborhood, and now after years of neglect another Kingston ghetto. Mark and other young Rastas awaited the legendary Gilly Dread's arrival. Not having seen his father in more than a decade, Mark was obviously proud of introducing Gilly to his friends. We met just outside Mark's house, where these enterprising youths had built a small bar where they could gather in the cool hours of the night, sharing talk and laughter after a hard day's work.

As the eastern sky began to lighten, I reminded Gilly I had an appointment with Seaga in a few hours. Mark had offered lodging, but I was exhausted and asked if we could still check into a hotel. So with the rising sun, bleary-eyed and heads drooping, we found a hotel and the receptionist accommodatingly gave us both a suite.

Feeling refreshed after a luxuriant shower, but with no time to sleep, I prepared for the interview. I called Gilly early to ensure that he would awaken in time for my appointment with the Honorable Edward Seaga, the man some Jamaicans believe is

RasTa Time

the devil incarnate and others view as the savior of Jamaican culture.

Unfortunately, Gilly got lost on the way, and we arrived half an hour late—precisely the amount of time Seaga had allotted for the interview. As I raced out of the car and up the steps to Seaga's office, Gilly said, "Don't worry, babe. He'll vibe with you!"

I apologized profusely to the former prime minister, who then cautiously offered the chair opposite him. Two hours later I left with an autographed copy of Seaga's latest book and his private number, in case I had any further questions. Gilly was right; we had vibed, and the Honorable Mr. Edward Seaga gave me a memorable interview.

Kathy Arlyn Sokol

EDWARD SEAGA INTERVIEW

RasTa Time

KAS: To millions of people around the world the photo of you, Bob Marley and Michael Manley onstage shaking hands….

Edward Seaga:
Hands up in the air, yes.

KAS:….at the One Love Concert in 1978 represents the kind of peace that Bob was trying to achieve. What was that moment like for you personally, and what effect, if any, did that event subsequently have on Jamaican politics?

Edward Seaga: First of all, it was unexpected. I didn't expect that Bob was going to make that move or to call on us, but it wasn't anything that could not have been achieved, and we complied. It was a moment of great excitement for the crowd, extreme excitement, because people felt that Bob was someone who was admired and stood so high in the community, on both sides of the political divide, and could have an impact on those who were not in agreement with each other, who were hostile to each other. And therefore this was an opportunity in which he could have made a big difference.

Well, he did make a difference. No question about it. But it didn't last too long because the divide was much deeper than what could be covered by a song. Although it was a very moving and particular song relevant to the occasion and the purpose, and the moment wasn't wasted by any means. It is still remembered, and as a result of that, the song 'One Love' has become something of an informal anthem of the country. People sing it a lot of times when there is a suitable occasion. So Bob Marley has left something indelible.

KAS: Did that moment in any way influence your notions of politics?

ES: I wouldn't say that Bob introduced those notions. He just reinforced them, but there are deeper concerns within the political system whether it is in the form of governance or in other areas of anomalies that will always be in the forefront of the mind. Whereas the theme of peace and one love is something that is at the back of the mind and comes forward at relevant times.

KAS: As I was driving here I saw the words One Love painted vertically down the side of a building. It seems that the effect that Bob Marley has had on Jamaica and the world is profound.

Did you have any indication at the time of that concert some 33 years ago that Bob Marley would become the national icon, and not just the national icon but representative of Jamaica throughout the world?

RasTa Time

ES: Bob had attained a certain elevated status from the early 70s. Once he started to sing reggae music and to compose reggae music he fitted in with the musical movement of the time, and it was a mutually beneficial thing. He helped to make reggae music a worldwide-accepted form of music and something that people delighted in hearing and dancing to, and that in turn made him. So with that mutual benefit both music and Bob Marley advanced.

We didn't at that time expect him to go much further than being a super star, because that is where everyone else ends. But, of course, in much later years long after he died, 20 years after he died, the accolades from the New York Times and from the BBC about the song *One Love* and the album *Exodus* gave a tremendous fillip to his status.

One Love was selected as the best song of the century, and *Exodus* the best album of the century. It was something that no one else could achieve. It was something so exceptional that it made Bob Marley a much bigger person, much greater person, with a greater impact than we had ever expected.

KAS: *Do you think that the vision and message of Bob Marley, this idea of One Love and Peace, has actually permeated the fabric of Jamaican society?*

ES: This is a kind of message that is pretty normal in the folk philosophy of the country. Peace is always desirable. One love is a good thing, so that is not something new. It is just good to hear it from the lips of someone who had the esteem that Bob Marley had, and especially when it is wrapped up by such musical lyricism and rhythm, etc. into a very attractive song. As I said it is not a profound statement. It becomes profound only because it is Bob Marley who made it.

KAS: *What has been the impact of Bob Marley on Jamaica?*

ES: He is still a very revered person, still a very admired person for his musical talents and his performances. He didn't just sing. He was a superb performer on the stage. His music is played very often and he is still the subject of discussions. In all those respects it has kept him alive as if he is still here.

In villages, in cities, in towns across the globe Bob Marley's name is known, and to that extent he is a worldwide figure and therefore not one who is limited to just his local impact.

KAS: How has the popularity of Rastafarianism impacted the country?

ES: There are all kinds of Rastafarian people. There are people who treat it as a genuine religious movement, and they are very serious about what they do and their beliefs. Then there are others who assume the high psychological profile of the Rasta into form of dress, and what they eat, and how they talk because it suits whatever background or career they are in, like the music business. The Rastas are creative people and they have become involved in the emergence of Jamaican music because of their creativity, and now there are others who emulate them in the expectation that this will help them to become a part of that type of movement.

Now I know that Bob Marley was one of those that took Rastafarian religion as something serious. He was distinct from the others who are using the veneer of Rastafarianism.

Kathy Arlyn Sokol

KAS: Were you a fan of Reggae music when it first emerged?

ES: Always. I think Jamaican music of the period-- the Ska, the Rock Steady, the Reggae and the DJ Music are all beautiful music. I would compare them with the most beautiful music anywhere else in the world.

RasTa Time

KAS: Do you have a personal favorite Bob Marley song?

ES: Yes, 'Redemption Song.' That was his last song. It was done in February of 1981. I think it symbolizes and encapsulates Bob Marley. When he spoke of the pirates—(recites)

> *Old pirates, yes, they rob I*
> *Sold I to the merchant ships*

— he is speaking about not just the exploiters of slaves, but of all exploiters. That was what Bob Marley did. He did not involve himself in the type of music and lyrics that others did. He lifted it out of that level into a higher level of the folk philosophy, a folk philosophy that impacted on a world of folk societies, a world of poor people, a world of vulnerable people, and a world where people are exposed through their vulnerabilities to the weaknesses that they can be exploited by. And that song really went to the center of everything that he was attacking and against. And when you put that kind of thinking in music it is a lot more powerful than when you put it in a book.

ROHAN MARLEY

Gilly introduced me to Rohan Marley, born on May 19, 1972, the son of Bob and Janet Hunt, as he was sitting outside at a table with a computer set up in front of him. He wanted to oversee the new businesses he had just launched under the Marley name, while still keeping an eye on the soccer game in progress. Once a professional football player, Rohan, like all the Marley boys, likes to keep fit.

Courtesy Gail Zucker

RasTa Time

I sat down next to Rohan and explained my mission, then asked if he could talk for a while.

He said that he had come to just vibe with the family, and that he hadn't expected to do an interview, but that we would talk later. He went off to play a few rounds of soccer, then sauntered over and placed a small square Rasta-colored purse on the table in front of me. I opened it and inside was a set of beautifully handcrafted earbuds made from bamboo, recycled plastics and a gold-plated connector. The earbuds were a sample of the House of Marley audio collection of personal electronics and accessories, which Rohan had just test-launched the month before.

I placed them in my ears and listened with crystal clarity, as this son of Bob Marley, himself the father of seven children, five of them with Grammy-award winning hip-hop artist Lauryn Hill, spoke of the values he had learned from his father and was now passing on to the next generation. These are the same values and principles, he says, that he applies to the worldwide distribution of Marley Coffee, another of his recent enterprises. The coffee is grown on his 52-acre all-organic farm atop the Blue Mountains in Jamaica, where the farmers who tend the land must adhere to strict organic principles and the Ital standard — natural, pure and from the Earth.

RasTa Time

ROHAN MARLEY INTERVIEW

Kathy Arlyn Sokol

KAS: Today at 56 Hope Road on the anniversary of your father's passing there was a celebration of life. A 'Positive Vibration.'

RM: That is true. When you have life, you have for certain an opportunity to do things, you know. Cause once you can breathe, you have a chance to do anything here in this physical realm.

It is an awakening, you know. It's people accepting a way of life. People wanting to love and people just loving, you know. In this awakening, the first thing is, you have to accept yourself, accept who you are. Yeah. You have to accept what you are as a person and you have to accept life in general, you know. That stage is what you call self-love; love within yourself. You first have to know what love is before you can speak of love.

RasTa Time

We are all connected. Tree has life just like I have life. So we all are connected. The goal is really to focus on that development. We are all connected to the universe and we are all planted here on earth and we are all receive one vibration. This is the earth vibration. Naturally if the vibration is positive and you have a positive direction to a cause, you can make a positive change.

It can't be just for self-gain, self-fulfillment, or it won't work. It is about the bigger picture; about bringing your strength and focus to a place where you can make a change and create more opportunity. So that is the vibration. If the vibration is not positive from where it start in the head then you can imagine the rest of the thing. So the head have to have the focus.

RasTa Time

KAS: *I watched as you and your brothers played soccer today. The sun is shining, the weather is oh so sweet... It is a truly magic day as people around the world give remembrance...*

RM: What you see today is how we desire to be everyday which is live in love and joy. So that is just our natural habits, you know. These things we do as a life. As we live, we do things to keep the energy going, things to recharge the battery and to illuminate ourselves, you know. You have to get the cells going, to really wake up the cells, so you can activate the blood to go a little faster. More current, more energy. That is why it is good to do these things. The more energy you excrete, the more energy you gain.

KAS: *You are the father of seven children. What lessons do you share with your children that you learned from your father?*

RM: Truth. He was telling us the truth for us to see it. I obviously got a father who was for his children. He gave the truth to my generation, and I must do the same thing and so must my brothers, you know. It continues with each generation. The next generation will see more of the truth, and that is great. It is wonderful that one is willing to learn the truth of reality and accept it as it is.

Live and have no fear.

Discipline. Discipline means to be still, so you can hear. Once you can hear then you can know, but if you are not hearing then you cannot know. So that is what is important.

Be respectful to your elders. Respect others.

Be physically strong and the more you grow, the more you will learn.

You don't want to overbog them with too much because they have to go to school, but the most important thing is the truth. They all know Rastafari, which is our way of life. Of course, with today's technology they can do their own research and learn from their own selves and keep on going, but still they remember the original teaching that they get.

KAS: How do you view this moment and what is your vision for the future?

RM: The view of the moment is what you see. Brothers and sisters living in harmony, you know, and that is the future.

KAS: *You have taken the Marley legacy in a new direction with the establishment of Marley Coffee. In what ways does Marley Coffee help further your father's vision?*

RM: We just happened to gain the opportunity to grow another part of the mind, which is to really get involved in the earth, you know, in a physical sense by developing a farm. You have a certain amount of land space, but how do you take that land and reach out to the entire universe? How can this little piece of land become relevant? What is the purpose of it? What are you going to do with it? Why is it?

When I looked out, I realized the importance of coffee to many farmers throughout the world. I saw coffee beans, coffee drinks, coffee as a commodity. We had the land and we had this commodity. So there were no limitations in my mind as to how I can learn to develop the coffee from the first state, the cherry state, all the way to the packaging. I just wanted to expand my mind. I saw something that could grow both on the land and in my mind.

It also creates opportunity for other people, you know, jobs. The goal is to really develop the community because those people have been living on that land for longer than I have. So I am able to create more opportunity for the community and make the place more vibrant and give it a longer life.

The first thing for me was that the coffee had to be organic. We wanted our coffee to be ital and based on the principles of Rastafari. Our farm is growing in a sustainable way, so that when I go to the land, I can see the farmers joyful and happy because they are building their community and a lifestyle, the Marley lifestyle, which is you have to give to receive.

My father taught us the values of Haile Selassie I, the First, His Majesty, about the way of life and how to live. Dealing in that way of life, you naturally become earthly. You think earth first and connect to the earth. It make no difference who you are. It is how you are, and that is how we treat each other on the farm. My father say that one day he is going to stop playing music and just farm. I am that. I am the other side.

Mitsuhiro Sugawara

RasTa Time

RasTa Time

Kathy Arlyn Sokol

JULIAN MARLEY

Julian 'Ju Ju' Marley, tall, lean, and muscled for agility, is Bob's son with Barbadian beauty Lucy Pounder. He was born on June 4, 1975, just the day before his father launched the Wailer's *Natty Dread* Tour. Bob's only son born in England, Julian spent his early years between his mother's base in London and visiting the Marley home in Kingston, finally settling in Jamaica in 1993 to be closer to his brothers and sisters.

On one visit to Kingston, when Julian was only 5 years old, he presented his family with his own-recorded version of "Slave Driver," one of his father's classics from the Wailers' first album released on Chris Blackwell's Island label, *Catch A Fire,* in 1973, which established them as international stars.

A precocious musical prodigy, Julian taught himself keyboard, bass, drums and guitar, and made his international début at the age of 14 with his album, *Uprising,* named after his father's last tour with the Wailers. Keeping his father's music alive, he feels, is what he was ordained to do, and he works to maintain the spirit of his band as well. He continues to collaborate with original Wailers like Bunny

Wailer, Tyrone Downie and Aston 'Family Man' Barrett, whose son, Aston Jr., was a founding member of Julian's own band, also named *Uprising*.

Throughout his now 36 years, the age Bob Marley was when he passed away, Julian has devoted himself to carrying on his father's message and musical legacy. He strongly identifies with his Jamaican heritage, but he also feels privileged to be part of the next generation of British-born reggae artists, and to continue the musical roots that his father put down in England.

As a major supporter to the Ghetto Youths Foundation, Julian also gives back to Jamaica by helping struggling youth in communities across the island. Wherever he travels and performs in the world, his music offers positive guidance, singing his songs as wake-up calls to all. Inspiration, he believes, rules the earth.

Julian says that he never plans the next step; he just continues with the work of Ras Tafari, and things just come together naturally. And true to his belief, our chance conversation flowed as easily as the dreadlocks down his back.

RasTa Time

Beat Magazine Courtesy Roger Steffens

Kathy Arlyn Sokol

JULIAN MARLEY INTERVIEW

RasTa Time

***KAS:** Today on May 11, 2011, we stand in front of a mural of your father at 56 Hope Road, once his residence and now the Bob Marley Museum. Many have gathered to pay respects to your father on this day of his passing. What do you feel from this moment?*

JM: What I feel is alive in the spirit of Life and in the spirit of our father because I feel him everyday. We take Bob Marley as a godly person, so we talk about God and life and righteousness. And we know that spirit live on. It feels good and I want to tell you we are here on other days too, so today is just another day that we are here.

Our father's spirit has never left here. So to be here and to be inspired spiritually as well as musically, you know....Inspiration rule earth, you know, inspiration controls earth; it is hard to even explain it really. It is like an ordained feeling, as if we are ordained to carry on his message.

Today I get to see some other brethren that I have not seen for a long time, many which happen also to be some of our father's friends, so it is a special day. But it is a natural feeling for me, you know what I mean, because every day is a 'Gong' day for me.

Today is just living, yes. I think about what is light, the sunshine, not the darkness. There is always light, and that is what we are facing here today on Hope Road—sunshine, beauty, nature and cool breeze, you know. We have food and we drink some juice and smoke some herb too, yeah. (Laughs) So today is a beautiful day and we are in a congregation of Rasta.

Today we have lots of young ones around and they are at where? Bob Marley House. And what does Bob Marley represent? Righteousness and equality. So just being here in the presence of Rasta is great in itself, you know what I mean? That is the right place to be…yeah…

RasTa Time

KAS: *We watch all these Marleys playing soccer as we talk. Do you remember coming to this place as a young boy?*

JM: Yes, I first started coming here when I was around five. I would come every summer vacation and every school holiday. But it was different then, even the buildings. You used to be able to walk straight through the wall here. The yard was more open. You would come back around here and there would be a wood fire with food cooking. It was a different nature, not as much concrete, more natural.

As little youths, there would be big men playing soccer in the yard, and I would watch them. You would see different faces like Carlton Barett and his brother, Family Man. We would have seen a lot of a great ones, you know, who are not even here today, but we can remember. But even if you remember things as a little youth it is different, you know. My imagination back then was about adventure. Now me come, everything relaxed, so me feel a different feeling today.

KAS: *You were born in London. Did you ever feel separate from the other brothers?*

RasTa Time

JM: Noooo. How can I be separate? Only in the sense that we are all born separate. I came out of my father line and this is my father's house. How can I be separate? We were all created by the same father.

KAS: You speak of being in the presence of Rasta. Part of the Rasta tradition is the smoking of herb or marijuana. Your father called it the 'healing of the nation.' What is the significance of marijuana in your life?

JM: Our father told you already. It is about raising your consciousness, your awareness. It is a plant that was here long before we humans were. So who are we to talk about whether it is legal or not? It exists. God make creation and if God make creation He never make no mistake in creation. He never make no bush that has no use at all. Whether it is to look at, or to create oxygen or boil some tea out of it, or you eat from it or you smoke of it or you drink of it. The earth provide everything.

But every day babies are born into the world to work. You are given a number and have to follow the system and do what the system make you do. We learn this through education and all that stuff and are programmed like this from birth. Then you reach to be a big man and become an adult and you find so many hardships and don't have a moment for yourself because your mind is full of bills, wake up to go to school, to work, and when nighttime come, the day is gone and you have no time for yourself. And everyday goes like that; sometimes people live their entire lives like that. Every day.

The herb now give you a moment, even if it is only for five minutes, within those five minutes you can be easy and meditate. What has a problem has a solution. It is the healing of the nation.

We need a healing from the sufferation that go on and the sufferation is mental. You check it out everyone still can eat food for the belly, but the mind is under torment. Babylon. The herb free up that, you know?

***KAS** : Your father said that 'the revolution will not be televised. It will be telepathic and that there will be nothing that can stop it.' He believed that it was this generation that would carry the revolution forward. But isn't the younger generation overwhelmed by the continual devastation wrought by Man and by Nature?*

JM: Youth them want the knowledge but not given the knowledge, you know in this time and age. I don't know well why for destruction causes? That don't make no sense. So in this present time we need my father's message and we have to respect the forefathers who set the way. Then we can be who we are — speak with freedom and speak of all these great things.

Sometimes we go through hard times, tough times, detrimental times, but you know there is a creator who is one divine creator... once we know there is a creator we have a faith. If you don't know there is a creator you would be frightened everyday of your life. And me, I live every day knowing that there is a defender for I and I, and that is God himself. See when you have that defense, you have a feeling that there is hope and that there will be a way. So, the whole thing is to let love be your way, you know? Yes, let love be the way...

Fear is a thing, you know, but obviously if anything is going to happen, it will happen. So maybe that means you don't need the fear.

But definitely this time we are living in... first of all, I am on Gideon time, you know, which is Biblical time, Revelation time. The revolution is not televised and it hasn't been talked about and it is telepathic and it start already, you know. Maybe people don't see it as a revolution, but it is.

We speak of Africa Unite. And that is what we really, really want. Them call it a continent because they bust it all up in a million pieces but me call it a country. And if Africa unite you will see a big change around the world, I tell you the truth. That energy will spread universally, you know. Ethiopia was the genesis of all humankind...This whole thing is sometimes not easy to talk about, but it is something once you see, you can understand it. Once you see all that is at risk, you can understand it still.

KAS: The colonization of Africa and the consequent dissection of its land has been the root of endless warfare.

JM: Yes, and it is about we ourselves as people knowing what is best for us as people. Not just our governments can talk, we the people must say, 'we would like it to be like this.' It takes people to make a change. We need the people because it is all about the people and everything is for the people. You know, that is what they say 'government for the people and by the people.' So, if we are not satisfied then we people must make the change. It is a big thing, you know what I mean?

RasTa Time

KAS: Your father sung about the mystic. How does the mystic work in your life?

JM: The mystic is natural and is something that everyone can feel, but you have to open up your heart to it. When we say open up the heart it means you have to be neutral with the earth, you have to be neutral with your brothers and sisters, and with the people of the earth. A lot of people like to be enclosed, like they are afraid of life, you know what I mean?

The natural mystic is that we are all created by one creator. The mystic is God's creation and it is so right in front of our face that we don't see it. It is love. When we speak of love we speak of one thing. There may be love between a man and a woman or amongst a family, but what about the love that is here right now? The mystic is about your heart, heart and heart. All hearts beating as one. No division is there. Man makes division and God waits.

KAS: With all that you have been given in life, how do you give back?

JM: Our father sing 'unity' is the key. What we are giving into this world is the Word of God or Word of Rastafari, the Word of peace and unity. I give thanks that we were born in the Light of God, Rastafari, which gives us even more strength. Anything we speak is about righteousness. Therefore we have the power and the strength to back us. We say 'herb, love, unity, Africa unite....' Your own mind and your own commonsense tell you what is right and what is not right.

It is a continuation of Life at every moment, and it comes down the generations the same way. Everyday a new baby born and a new generation coming up, and then the music changes. Right now the best thing I can put out is more positive words in music because to reach out to the masses of people individually is impossible, but through the music possible.

The passion of my music is delivering the message to the people. The time is at hand now when we will see the revelation of great things. That is my driving force everyday —— to spread God's Word to the people. Everyday have new people, so everyday there is works to do, you know. It is stressful work but the music is what we love and we love to speak of righteousness. So, it's a joy.

We really give back from the gathering of the people, you know. It is like we are talking right here right now, so someone might read this interview and maybe get an inspiration. So it is because you are here today that other people are going to know what it is that we have to offer; and the morality of what we have to offer through our music and words. We don't have millions of dollars to offer. What we have is words for the soul, which is more than anything else in the whole universe.

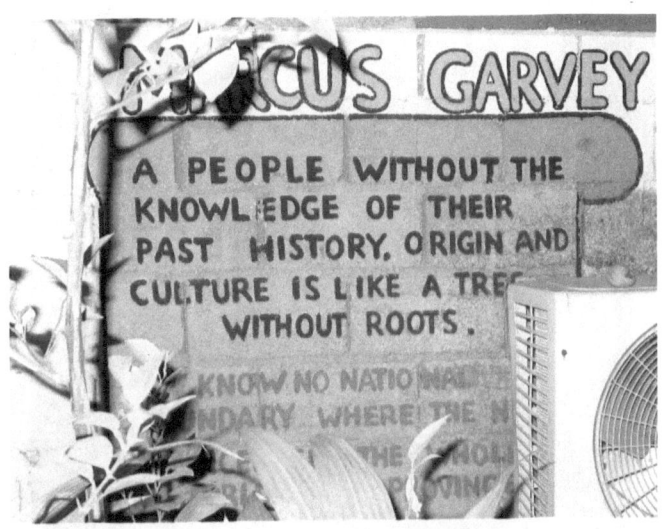

Kathy Arlyn Sokol

©*Mitsuhiro Sugawara*

BAHAMAS and DONISHA PRENDERGAST

By the time Gilly and I got back to the hotel, he had to rush me to the airport for my early morning departure to the Bahamas. Even when I reached Nassau, there wasn't a moment to spare. I placed my bags down in my hastily booked room and flagged a cab to the Bob Marley Resort & Spa, where I had arranged to meet Donisha Prendergast.

We had barely introduced ourselves before Donisha led me into another car, in which the director and cameraman of her film *Rasta: A Soul's Journey* were waiting to be driven to the airport. After we delivered them and they ran for their plane, I was finally alone with Donisha and plunged into our interview, knowing that in a couple of hours she also had to catch a flight.

Donisha was born on December 29, 1984, to Rita Marley's daughter, Sharon, whom Bob had adopted when he and Rita married, and Peter Prendergast, Jamaica's best known and highly respected soccer referee. Besides famous heritage on both sides of the family, she has also earned a proud name of her own as an actor, poet, film director, activist and model.

Like most Marleys, music has been a natural part of Donisha's everyday life. When still a babe, Donisha was carried along by her mother, Sharon, who was then touring with the Melody Makers, the group that she had formed with brothers Ziggy and Stephen, and sister Cedella. At home on stage and in front of the camera, Donisha has starred in several Jamaican theatrical productions, hosted the island's wildly popular version of 'American Idol,' and is featured on billboards and in magazines across the Caribbean. She has even done some collaborative work with her grandmother, including Rita Marley's video "*Take me To the West Indies*."

Having grown up in a family that sustained her grandfather's legendary devotion to Rastafari, Donisha set off on a new path at the age of 22 to explore the world of Rastafari for herself. Her travels took her to Ethiopia, South Africa, India, Israel and islands throughout the Caribbean. The five-year odyssey culminated in the documentary, *Rasta, A Soul's Journey,* which examines the roots and diverse cultural expressions of the Rastafari movement and its global impact.

RasTa Time

Courtesy Patricia Scarlett

Donisha is clearly "the next generation" that Bob Marley referred to in our interview -- an emboldened supporter of truth, love and justice for all. She spoke passionately of her sense of mission, each word intense with ardor and authenticity. We talked for so long that she missed her flight…

Kathy Arlyn Sokol

DONISHA PRENDERGAST INTERVIEW

RasTa Time

©Che Kothari

KAS: What was special and distinctive about your upbringing?

Donisha: Apart from the fact that we never really spoke in words; we really sang music? Whenever my family would have an argument, we would resolve it with conversations, but conversations through music. We'd play some of my grandfather in the house, "Lion of Judah" and that would mellow out the vibes and then we would be able to talk. (Laughs)

Those are the nice parts of my childhood. We had a good experience – I never wanted for anything when I was growing up. What I did want was more time with my mother because she was always on the road traveling. Grandma would always be coming this weekend but she would never reach because she always had somewhere else to go. At this age I can understand it because I, too, always have somewhere else to go and am missing moments with my younger brothers and sisters.

But it is for a purpose; it is for a mission. A more global perspective than even the eyes can see. The heart feel it, my spirit feel it. Everyday when I wake up there is so much work to do. Some days I have a schedule, but then other days it is like the positive energy just take you to do the work.

Courtesy Michael Chambers

Kathy Arlyn Sokol

Courtesy Michael Chambers

KAS: In the interview I did with your grandfather, he says, 'it is the Truth that keeps it going and what you feel inside, and to know that you are doing it for a purpose.' How do you interpret his purpose, his mission, and how was it instilled in you?

Donisha: I understand it more and more everyday by just looking around me. Mission, mission, mission. Mission is just a word to explain the things that are missing in this world. The mission is to fill those things that are missing – love, healing, perspectives on the self before you judge another man, justice, truth and rights. That is the mission because those are the things that are missing. We are not living in a perfect world, so let us not be disillusioned. There is no way that we can make this world perfect either, but there are many holes that we can fill so simply.

KAS: How does your work reflect the ideals of your grandfather's message?

Donisha: I decided to give my life to Rastafari and all that means—to the service of people, service to Truth, and carrying out my grandfather's message. Even beyond that just being brave enough to do this thing he was talking about and find this one love.

One love. What does one love truly mean? Can we all really be one people? Can we all have a united vision, united sense of each other? It must be. This passion that I feel inside of me is too hot to be made up.

KAS: *Your grandfather told me that the revolution will not be televised it will be telepathic so nothing can stop it, and that it is the next generation, your generation, who will move it forward. Do you feel empowered to be the generation that leads the way?*

Donisha (laughing): I am of a different generation. I am of a different breed. It is a lot of responsibility but I feel very ready. I am very capable, I am very inspired because my mother never raised me as a child my entire life. I imagine that these are the days that she was raising me for. This is the mission she prepared me for.

I just want some help. I just want brothers and sisters to be brave enough to love and really understand, really 'overstand', what love means. You can't just think love. It is a weird thing to try to explain how you can have this intense love for a stranger; how you can just feel so much pain and so much responsibility for somebody you don't know.

That is love. That feeling. It is also action. Action is love. You can't say you love me and be afraid to hug me. You can't say you love me and point me in the face of war.

What are these leaders dealing with? I wonder what my grandfather would have said.

I am much less tolerant of so many things around the world. Experience does that, but also choice. You choose not to be as tolerant about certain things, you know? My grandfather chose not to be tolerant about a lot of things, but he did it in a way that was healing and wasn't offensive. He sang it with melodies and music, you know, and they killed him. I know that.

KAS: *Why do you think they killed him?*

Donisha: Why do I know? Because it can't make sense to me. If you look at the story that history tells – all of the great ones are taken down. They don't fall. They are taken down. How can we be led into comfortably believing that this man died so simply from something that can be treated? I just have a real difficulty in believing it.

I have heard the story all my life – he broke his toe playing football and it turned into cancer and spread into his brain and killed him. I hear the story but what is the truth? I try not to think about those things too much because it makes me very upset.

KAS: But at the same time you feel that your grandfather's presence is here.

Donisha: I know that his presence is here. All of us feel him presence, him presence don't leave us. Everyday the music even if it is not on the radio, it is coming from somebody's mouth.

KAS: Wherever you go around the world.

Donisha: Yeah mahn, yeah mahn. Today we are able to go on the Internet and learn about Bob Marley and see his picture and hear his music, but we are not able to see Bob Marley, and so we think we don't feel his energy. And the message sometimes is lost behind the image and behind the excitement of the music. All of these great things like the rebel of the music and the rebel of the movement and the rebel of the man...

I never knew my grandfather in the physical. I never met him like you. I never exchanged words with him, but I can't deny him. I can't deny that I know him. There is something that is living beyond me that is coming through me, that is not of me and I just have to be open and be a vessel to it and let it come through, because the works have to continue.

There is so much work to do. The people are still hungry. People are still dying from injustice. There is still greed. Our eyes are open and they are doing it in front of our eyes. Have we no voice? I take it personal, because my grandfather died for this. Leaders died for this. Mothers cry for this. And I am just tired of waiting to see someone come forth and do something and be brave enough to say certain things and I pray for guidance and protection everyday, but the work has to be done.

KAS: You just listened to an excerpt of the interview I posted on YouTube for your grandfather's birthday. In it he says that '....You have to respect what you feel of this atmosphere, love and respect creation. And then you start search you will find Rastafari.' You are now doing a film on Rastafari around the world...

Donisha: When you start search you will find Rastafari (laughs)....That is exactly what is happening right now.

To be very honest with you, when I was growing up I never heard about Rastafari, I always heard about Bob Marley. Growing up in the Marley family, people treat you like a Marley. They don't treat you like a Rasta, because being a Marley and being a Rasta are two different things. It is as if Bob Marley stands alone as a Rasta, but he doesn't.

Courtesy Michael Chambers

After traveling the world trying to discover the roots and evolution of Rastafari and opening myself to that experience, it gave me a totally different perspective of life. I am now a different person and I have a different inspiration. Rastafari guide me every day.

KAS: What are you personally discovering in your search for Rastafari?

Donisha : We have been working on this film for about six years and been traveling for about four. It has been an amazing journey around the world like you said in search of Rastafari, but you can't really search for Rastafari. So even the title of the film and the whole mission changed because when I started on this journey I was in search of Rastafari and what I came upon was myself.

Courtesy Patricia Scarlett

I hear people saying them searching for themselves, but I say just know yourself. If you are searching for yourself then who have you been living with all of these years? Know yourself and accept yourself. It is hard. It is hard to look in the mirror and say the things that are not good and are not right about you, yet it is something that everyone should practice.

I realized that you can't search for anything. Because the Truth just is. You just have to acknowledge it and believe in it. Whether it is a good or a bad truth, whether the leaders have lied to you or you have been lying to yourself.

There is so much illusion in this world. What we must know is that nothing that we see is real. Nothing that we see is real until you feel it.

There is strength inside of every single solitary one of us; strength that you don't know about until it is called upon. Have faith in that. I have always had a love for people and people have always had a genuine love for me, and their love has made me fearless in a way that many can't understand.

As cliché as it may sound to others, I feel like I have to be a bridge. I realize that I have access to a lot of resources, a lot of networks, and know a lot of people. People look towards me because of who my grandfather is, and associate different images in their head of who I must be, and these things can be used in a positive way. It is almost like Robin Hood (laughs) – *get from the rich and give to the poor* – and that is the role that I feel I must play in educating.

The education that the rich have the poor must have. The ability to turn their talent into something that can make them money to sustain themselves, they must have. The knowledge of how to heal yourself naturally with herbs and to eat a healthy diet, they must have. To know how to build their own industries, sustainable knowledge, they must have. I have access to these things. I am well educated, my family made sure of that, so wherever I am in the world I know I have work to do.

KAS: As an educated, well-known, and influential individual you can utilize those things to bring his message forward on a level that will gain greater respect.

Donisha: I have to. His Imperial Majesty Rastafari himself said, 'it is the duty of the educated few to fulfill the legitimate aspirations of the uneducated many. Many will be called but only a few chosen.'

Like I said earlier it is about being a bridge, especially for the young people, the generation that comes after me, who is caught up in this technology thing. We now have to find a way to communicate with the ones who need to hear.

RasTa Time

KAS: Your grandfather also said, 'if you do not know that it is not right from early, later is going to be too late because you can't bend an old tree, might as well chop it down, but if it is a young tree you can steer it... 'How is the message of his music manifesting in this generation?

Donisha: By the change in people's lifestyle. The way them live everyday. That is how we know the music is manifesting. Once people change them lifestyle that means they are open to certain things. Check this, Rastafari teaches you to eat healthy, to live good with your brother and your sister, to seek justice, to use your voice to stand up for equal rights at all times, and to always walk with the spirit.

My journey has already shown me that things are moving, and that his music has manifested a respect for life. Everywhere I go around the world, I see Rastas. Them live on an organic farm outside of the bounds of society. Them home-school them children, them grow them herb, and them hail their Emperor. I look at this guy and see a white man with orange hair and freckles, and ask how it is that you can identify with Rastafari?

Him tell me it is through the music. The music don't see color, the music don't see race, the music just communicates experience and a philosophy of life. That is what is manifesting through him, so I know that my grandfather's words never died. They are living now more than ever.

KAS: What songs of your grandfather's give you the most inspiration?

Donisha: *Jah Live*. Jah Live is one of my favorite songs from my grandfather because it is like a prayer. (sings)

> ***Fool say in their heart***
> ***Rasta your God is dead***
> ***But I and I know Jah***
> ***Jah Live children, yeah.***

Your God is not dead. Nobody has left you. We must keep building. This is just the battle. There have been battles that have been fought many years ago for these days, and in these days we must fight those battles for those days to come.

Like my grandma explained to me. She said when your grandfather sang, *No Woman, No Cry* " hush little darling, don't shed no tears" meant hush, you are a woman, not a baby, so woman no cry. Have strength. Him not empathizing with the woman.

Him saying the woman have a role and a responsibility, and he is trying to strengthen us.

Courtesy Ashlee Hutchinson

Courtesy Ashlee Hutchinson

He is just observing life and then realizes that this is what woman was born to do – bear pain. When that time of the month comes we get cramps. I have never seen a man getting cramps yet. When we are giving birth, there is pain. And as women, we feel more emotional pain.

I understand it a little bit more now about role and responsibility as a woman and I don't cry as much I guess, for little things, at least.

RasTa Time

KAS: How do you see the kind of responsibility that you and your grandmother carry in bringing the message of your grandfather forward as women compared to the men in the Marley family? Is there a difference?

Donisha: Yeah man, there must be naturally because I am more open to the experience of people and strangers. Some may say it is naiveté but I think it is femininity. Women are naturally caregivers, nurturers, lovers.

Kathy Arlyn Sokol

We carry a lot, a lot, a lot of responsibility. We have the movement in our hands, that is the truth, because we are the braver ones. We are the ones who can heal, who can communicate and who are honest enough to tell the truth. We are the ones who carry the future in our bellies. So it is important for the woman, especially the Rasta woman, to know her role – and stand beside her king man, to cook and to clean in the house, but also to write at night, to read at night, to teach. These are the things that my grandmother and my mother have shown me.

On May 11th, my grandma had an event here at the Marley Resort and Spa. We as a family were celebrating thirty years of my grandmother's work; not necessarily thirty years since my grandfather has gone because my grandmother has done so much work in that time. My grandfather never lived to see any of it, but she is here and we have to give thanks for that.

RasTa Time

KAS: Here we sit in Bob Marley's home in the Bahamas, where he lived after he was shot in 1976 in Jamaica. Why is the message of this man, who is the emblem of peace and love and represents Jamaica around the world, not more resonant in the place in which it was born?

Donisha: Hypocrisy! Hypocrisy, and fear to do the right thing. Fear to not be in favor. Everybody lives in fear and I understand fear because I am one of those everybody. We must be conscious that in life everyone is feeling pain at all times. Everyone. We can't live just for ourselves 'cause then we never live.

RasTa Time

I hope by making these steps that I will not be walking alone because there are things that need to be said, and if I am to say it I want to know that there will be voices behind me. This is not about me; it is about something bigger than all of us. It is not by chance that I am a part of this family and that these things have been left for us to do. These things are not by chance.

I have great shoes to fill. So some say. But I say I walk in my own shoes, because we are on the same journey. Like my Uncle Ziggy say 'love is my religion'. Teach me that. It makes life so much easier…

Kathy Arlyn Sokol

RasTa Time

Donisha/KAS
(laughs and sings)
Help one another on the way and make it much easier, just a little bit easier…

Donisha: Selah.[3] Love is the easiest and the only way that we as a people, as individuals, as a world will ever heal. And by listening to some more of Bob Marley's music! (laughs).

KAS: What kind of youth movements are you personally involved in?

Donisha: There is an artist revolution on the rise, not just musicians, but filmmakers, painters, photographers, and writers who are all coming together now to go into the inner cities and teach them how to become filmmakers, painters, photographers, and writers. We have to empower each other through these things because we are all artists. Every one of us. Because we have all experienced life, and if we can find the artist inside of us, then everything would be all right. My

---

[3] **Selah** (Hebrew: סֶלָה, also transliterated as *selāh*) is a word used frequently in the Hebrew Bible, often in the Psalms, and is a difficult concept to translate. It is probably something like "stop and listen". " The Amplified Bible states Selah as "pause, and think of that". From Wikipedia

grandfather found the artist inside of himself. Yeah, (sings) *everything is going to be all right*.

We have all of these musicians and all of these people who have been able to make money and make moves up the ladder of society but have not looked back to give a hand to help others to move forward. And to them I say, 'put your money where your mouth is.' But there are also so many things that can happen without money. Life happens without money. Action, that is what I say. Build the schools. Go into the communities. Sit with the youth. Read with them.

You know there is so many things that we take for granted. I am 26 years old right now, and I am looking forward to having children. I am nervous about it because you know I hope I will do the best job, but it is important that we know that we are always raising children. We are responsible for all children. Not just when you give birth. Operate in that light, and this is how we will manifest these things.

Change something about how we have been programmed. Reeducate yourself because like I said what you see is not real, what you see is not the Truth. It is like Uncle Damien have a song, 'teachers will teach us,' but who teach the teacher? The preacher will bless us but who bless the preacher? Who writes the newspapers that you are reading? Who bottles the water that they feed you?' Questions, do the research, get active in your own life, and stop waiting on this figure to just come down from the sky and make everything all right.

KAS: Because heaven is here on the earth?

Donisha: We make heaven here on earth; this is our heaven right now. (sings)

> *But if you know what life is worth,*
> *You will look for yours on earth*
> *Now you see the Light...*
> *Stand up for your rights.*
> *Never give up the fight.*

My grandfather music guide me everyday. It is not just music. It is a philosophy of the way to live your Life.

RITA MARLEY

Donisha and I met early the next morning and again set off to the airport. This time, our driver was a sweet-natured young woman whom Donisha simply introduced as Auntie. I had no idea what that meant, since she appeared to be the same age as Donisha, who was 26.

As we sped to the airport, the three of us listened to the edited version of my Bob Marley interview, and Donisha began to cry. She said that she had longed to hear these words of her grandfather's and felt as if they had been spoken just for her.

At the airport, she jumped out of the car, I followed; we hugged, then she ran for her flight.

While driving back to my hotel, '"Auntie" revealed that my interview was the first time she had ever heard Bob Marley's spoken voice. I was bewildered. How can anyone living in the heart of this Rasta world not have heard a recording of Bob Marley speaking?

Auntie said that his words sent chills down her spine, that she wanted her mother and sister to hear the interview. As we exchanged numbers, she apologized for not having her own cell phone;

RasTa Time

instead, she gave me her mother's number and below it, this 'nameless' woman wrote down her own name: Serita Stewart.

It was not until I got back to my hotel room that I discovered that Serita is Rita Marley's youngest daughter, and the number that she had just given me was her mother's, Rita Marley's, private cell.

Exhausted by three sleepless days, I stepped out on the veranda of my 7th floor room to get some energy from the sun. When former Japanese Prime Minister Hatoyama's wife, Miyuki, had spoken on national television about her daily ritual of "eating the sun," she was ridiculed. But as I sat there taking in a mouthful of solar radiance, I felt gratifyingly restored. I then opened my eyes, looked up to the sky, and had what can only be called a '*daydream,*' as Rita Marley's face suddenly appeared, outlined by the sun.

I blinked twice, thought to myself: what was that? At that moment a red-legged thrush landed on the balcony railing, edged toward me and cocked its head as if trying to tell me something. I suddenly realized that I was waiting for Serita's call and had left my phone in the room. I slid the glass door open to the sudden sound of the phone ringing; I ran in, grabbed the phone and answered to Serita saying, "Please hold for Mrs. Rita Marley." Rita and I spoke for a few minutes, then she said: "Come tonight."

So in just a few hours, I was to meet the Marley clan matriarch, Alpharita Constantia Anderson Marley. Born in Cuba on July 25, 1946, Rita was brought to Jamaica by her parents when she was three months old. When she turned 8, her father, a carpenter by trade and a musician by preference, took her mother with him to England to look for work. Rita and her five brothers and four sisters were left behind in the care of various relatives.

Rita moved into her aunt's house, and at the age of 17 gave birth to her first child, Sharon. She took on nursing jobs to care for the infant, but Rita's real dream was to make it as a *ska* singer. She formed a female trio called the Soulettes, and when they appeared for an audition in 1964 at the studio where Bob Marley worked and recorded, Bob was assigned to be the group's mentor and rehearsal manager.

Soon Rita and Bob were a couple. In her autobiography, *No Woman, No Cry*, she writes that, *"We were so in love. Bob was so romantic and faithful, and I thought we would always be like that. We'd be rehearsing and looking into each other's eyes and singing, and then we'd put our mouths to each other's. It was magic."* They moved into a shed at the back of Rita's aunt's house, and on February 10, 1966, she and Bob Marley were married in a small ceremony held in a friend's living room. Rita was 19 and Bob had just turned 21.

Rita took care of Bob's professional and personal life, stoically accepting Bob's affairs with other women and the children they bore him; she often cared for the kids when they came to visit the Marley home at 56 Hope Road.

She and Bob had weathered some terrible storms, like the assassination attempt on their lives two days before the politically sensitive *Smile Jamaica* concert in 1976. Rifle-wielding assailants had burst into their home during a rehearsal for the event, intending to kill Bob, but the bullet only creased his breast below the heart and buried itself in his arm. Rita was running out of the house with the five Marley children when a bullet tore into her scalp and creased her skull.

The would-be assassins escaped. Despite the trauma, the decision was made to go on with the

Smile Jamaica performance. It was made so hurriedly that Rita appeared on stage alongside Bob dressed in a nightgown, with her bandaged head covered in a scarf.

Rita was again at Bob's side during the historic *One Love Peace Concert* in 1978, when he symbolically joined the hands of Jamaica's warring political rivals Prime Minister Michael Manley and opposition leader Edward Seaga.

Courtesy Jack Low

RasTa Time

Rita was also present at the momentous April 18, 1980, ceremony where Bob and the Wailers performed in celebration of the former British colony Rhodesia's rebirth as the independent state of Zimbabwe.

And Rita stayed strong at Bob's side during his final days in 1981, when the cancer had spread to his liver, lungs and brain.

Rita has never seen herself as a star, but as a mother, wife, sister and devout believer in the philosophy and tenets of Rastafari. With her husband's passing, she inherited the title of *Queen of Reggae* and found herself the Grand Dame of the Marley clan, assuming all its responsibilities with saintly patience and aplomb. As heir to the Marley legacy, she feels it is her mission to carry through the work that Bob began.

Knowing that time was precious, I arrived early for our meeting at the Bob Marley Resort and Spa to set up my recording gear. Rita was completely exhausted from the gala opening of the Spa, two days before, on the anniversary of her husband's passing, the launch of the Marley Mellow Drink on the same day and hosting a wedding party the following night. But she was totally gracious when she entered the room and embraced me with great warmth.

Rita sat down wearily, and I inserted into her ears the Marley House earbuds that Rohan had given me. I sat at her side and watched as she smiled and giggled, listening to the *EJ* version of my interview with her husband. When it finished, we began a brief but heartfelt exchange, sharing a deep respect for the wisdom of Bob Marley.

Afterward, she looked at me as Bob had that night at Shinjuku Kosei Nenkin Hall over 30 years ago and asked if I had been meditating on her today. I answered by telling her the story of eating the sun, her countenance outlined in its brilliance, and the bird alighting on my veranda, as if carrying a message from the skies. It was then, I continued, that I had walked into my room and received her call. She smiled and said, 'I heard your prayers. Welcome to 'Reality.'

RasTa Time

©*Mitsuhiro Sugawara*

Kathy Arlyn Sokol

Rita Marley Interview

RasTa Time

Courtesy Michael Chambers

KAS: I interviewed your husband in 1979 when Bob Marley and the Wailers toured Japan.

RM: I know your face.

KAS: I had lost the original interview with him and then suddenly after 30 years found an old cassette copy of it. Why I discovered it now is something that I am trying to understand.

RM: It is a fulfillment of his purpose here. His music and his words are going to get bigger and bigger until it reaches the right people. So there is a demand for that.

KAS: Did you ever expect that the message would grow in such a phenomenal way?

RM: Maybe if we had known we would have done it in a different way *(laughs)*. But we didn't know, so we were just doing it the way that Jah say, 'let it be done.' But if we had been planning for it and thought that it was going to go like this and go like that, I am sure that we would have done it in a different way. But this is Jah's way, where it just comes and flows. Freedom songs.... *sing these songs of freedom.*[4]

KAS: *Here on May 11th at the Bob Marley Resort & Spa you celebrated the release of the Bob Marley Mellow Drink .*

RM: It is significant in terms of it being a moment in time that comes once a year. We are not celebrating, we are more in memory of. It is past celebrating...we would celebrate his birth, but we are in memory of his passing. We are in memory of a man that lives, never dies.

His message continues to prove itself as reality. *One and all has to face reality.*[5]

The time that Japan is going through now is a world-wide crisis in different ways. Japan had it with water; some nations have it with fire. There are places burning and others flooding. Look at what is happening in America with all the tornadoes, and in Africa, too, there are problems.

---

[4] Lyrics from Redemption Song
[5] Lyrics from Natural Mystic by Bob Marley

So, Bob Marley's world never changes in terms of *'so much trouble in the world'.* *The way earthly thin's are goin, ' Anything can happen.*
So, all we gotta do is give a little, take a little.[6]
In other words, share — sharing and caring.

I hope that Japan takes the tsunami and earthquake they experienced seriously. This time they were hit by water, next time it could be by fire. *'It seems total destruction is the only solution.*[7]

So we all have to be on our p's and q's all over the world and unite ourselves as one people because that is the only way we can solve our problems. Uniting as one. Japan had this disaster with water. *This could be the first trumpet, might as well be the last*[8]....

All those proverbs and words that Bob sang about have meaning.

KAS: *His songs are prophetic and he is revered around the world as a king.*

---

[6]   Lyrics from So Much Trouble in the World
[7]   Lyrics from Real Situation by Bob Marley
[8]   Lyrics from Natural Mystic

RM: And a god. You were telling me that [when you were dancing at our concert and the ushers came and told you to sit down, you said to them that Bob was your *kamisama*, your god, and this was your way of praying to him]. There are many who believe like that and say that Bob Marley is their god and their King.

Courtesy of Michael Chambers

KAS: Do you remember anything special about your time in Japan?

RM: Yeah, mon, it was quite memorable in terms of us giving that love and that inspiration to people who it seems were hungering for it. They were starving for the reality of this man. They had heard about him before we got there, but they soon grasp his music and grow to love him. Then Japanese start wearing the red, green and gold; and wearing their hair in dreadlocks like Rasta trying to imitate him. It like Japan become more Rasta than even Jamaica. These are symbols for the youths around the world in terms of his teaching.

KAS: You have carried his name forward; you have borne his children and you have carried the responsibility of his legacy on your shoulders. Who is the man to you and how has his work become your work?

RM: It was just handed into my arms. It is like a relay race where you hand the baton to somebody else and they take it from you and they carry it to the next person until it get to the finale, to the end post. So, this is just my period with the baton and the mission continues; the struggle continues. There is no end until it is the end. Yeah?

'Until that day of lasting peace and world citizenship...[9]

I would love to live in Japan, and all over. When I go on tour and I see how beautiful God's world is, I would love to live in every part. World citizenship. "The Earth is The Lord's and the Fullness Thereof...."[10] That is a part of God's mission. But we are restricted because of boundaries and the wire fence. I am sure you have heard of Bob's interview where he says that there is no wire fence in his Father's kingdom. So, we have to move beyond the boundaries and the hurdles.

KAS: Could you tell us of your Africa Unite project?

RM: The Rita Marley Foundation works out of Ghana and we use Africa Unite as our slogan for the unification of all Africa, wherever. One of our missions is to bring unity, and what Africa Unite meant to Bob Marley and what it means to one and all. It is the only way out from what is going on right now.

---

[9] Lyrics from War
[10] Psalm 24:1 from the Bible

'War - war -Rumours of war....'[11]. It is only African unity that can solve it. Once Africa is united, the world unites because Africa is the strength of the world.

KAS: *Scientists have discovered remains of the earliest known human ancestors in Ethiopia.*

RM: Yes. Ethiopia was one Africa. It is that man came and divided it up. It was one Africa. One Ethiopia. There is the United States of America. We are trying to bring the United States of Africa. Unity. Unity is strength.

KAS: *Ethiopia is the birthplace of Emperor Haile Selassie I, Jah, Rastafari. When you were just a young girl, His Majesty visited Jamaica. What do you remember of that moment?*

RM: They say that seeing is believing, and I was able to see HIM as King of Kings, Lord of Lords, the Conquering Lion of the Tribe of Judah. Behold. Like they say, I behold HIM. That was my signal, and that was where my knowledge started to embrace who this man is and what the mission of Rastafari is. I learned by seeing HIM. It wasn't that

---

[11]   Lyrics from War

I didn't believe but seeing HIM was the greatest thing.

KAS: So that moment lives inside of you today?

RM: Oh, yes. What! It strengthens me. It gives me that reassurance that there is a God and He is a man. He is not a piece of stick. He is a man and that is good to embrace.

Beat Magazine Courtesy Roger Steffens

KAS: Jah Live is the first song that you and the I-Threes recorded with Bob.

RM: Yeah, mahn, that was one of Bob's special pennings. *Jah Live* was Bob's way of rebelling after they say that His Imperial Majesty was killed by Mengistu.[12] Bob said, No man, Haile Selassie can't be dead. Jah Live, and he went and penned that song and we sing backup.

That is how gifted Bob was. In his lifetime he was able to give predictions just like the prophets of old.

---

[12] Military junta leader who imprisoned and reportedly killed Emperor Haile Selassie I

Open the Bible and look in the Songs of David,[13] David the Musician, and how he interpreted his message through his music. And this is how the message come through Bob and his music.

KAS: Among the teachings that Bob shared with you, which do you feel are most important?

RM: The teachings of His Majesty, the teaching of God, the reading of the Bible. I learned a lot from that. We didn't have anything else to guide us through. That was our guiding light and still is.

When Bob was on stage he transcended into other heights. Sometimes we thought he would fly right

---

[13] These are the final words of David:
"The oracle of David son of Jesse,

the oracle of the man raised up as

the ruler chosen by the God of Jacob, 1

Israel's beloved 2 singer of songs:

23:2 The Lord's spirit spoke through me;

his word was on my tongue.

off the stage. This is why his music is so powerful thirty years after. He was lifted up by his spirit each time he went to perform, and each time I was standing by and it was apparent.

©*Mitsuhiro Sugawara*

KAS: *In my interview with Bob, he says, 'I'm in Jamaica and I make this record and it may be good for people and everybody get it, but I don't have to be there. So, it's just like the teachings of His Majesty, the philosophy, the ways of life, the example that Him set, that man should follow.'*

RM: Right, that is what I am saying. Bob's work is able to carry through without having to see him physically. There are people who have never seen him before and cherish his music. Youths, this generation; the generation just born they are saying , 'Bob Marley! We love Bob Marley.' It's amazing to know that even though they did not see him physically, they grew up loving him and listening to him, and loving him even more because they were deprived of seeing him physically.

KAS: You are the matriarch of a dynasty and oversee it all. How do you do it?

RM: Bob established this legacy, and I don't think about my responsibility. My assignment is assigned by God. I don't see myself as troubled about anything. I don't even think about it. So we just keep on going...

Just like you finish one chapter and you turn to another page and you take a deep breath and you say mission accomplished. But it don't finish, you know. We accomplish one thing but then there's more. Until it end there is no end to it. As I say, we just go with the flow...with no fear.

RasTa Time

FULL CIRCLE, LAWRENCE, KANSAS

With the completion of the interviews, we had the *heart* of the book, but were still in search of its face. One image of Bob Marley that would perfectly exemplify the book's title, *RasTa Time,* just happened to have been taken in Lawrence, Kansas, my hometown, and where my deep connection to Bob Marley first began. So, with nostalgic delight I set off for Lawrence, the last stop of my odyssey from LA to Miami to Jamaica to the Bahamas before returning to Japan.

On the same *Babylon by Bus* tour that I had interviewed Bob Marley in Tokyo in 1979, Richard Gwin, the *Lawrence Journal World* photo editor and an old friend, had captured an iconic image of Bob with dreadlocks flying wild as he danced onstage in bliss while performing at the University of Kansas' Hoch Auditorium.

After I arrived, Richard and I arranged to meet for lunch. When he came to pick me up at my brother's house, driving a red Ford station wagon bearing the license plate *BMarley, Kansas, The Heartland,* I knew I was truly home.

RasTa Time

Kansas is known as America's Heartland; its motto is *Home on the Range,* and its state animal is the courageous buffalo that once freely roamed the ranges in massive herds. Like King Sporty, Bob Marley, and the Buffalo Soldiers, Kansans, too, had adopted the buffalo as a symbol of strength and intrepid spirit.

Richard and I drove to his 5-acre farm just outside Lawrence, where his big picture windows look out upon golden wheat fields and his prized photo of Bob Marley hangs on the living room wall. But even before we entered the simple comfort of his Kansas farmhouse, I noticed a painting of Bob right

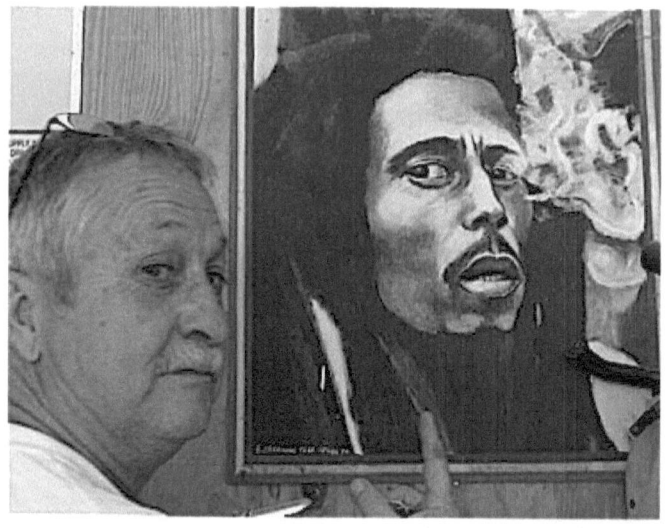

at the doorstep – and on the opposite wall, the companion to Richard's license plate, which reads: *BMarley ...Kansas, Home on the Range.*

Richard paused before we entered, took the license plate off the wall and presented it to me. "Bob was the Messenger," he said, "but you are the Deliverer. So please take this as a symbol of my support of your efforts to spread his message."

RasTa Time

I was moved by the gift, but also amazed at how deeply Bob had touched so many people in so little time. Time is, indeed, our greatest desire, and what Bob Marley and the Rasta Mystic have taught me, in this delightful decades-long journey, is that the human race is not meant to race 'against' time nor be ruled by time, but to find freedom and meaning 'in time' and to find completion in one another.

Armed with truth, grace and enduring lyrics, Bob Marley preached this message from stages around the world, recognizing that 'Reggae music is a music that can make you happy in a rebellious way…

Kathy Arlyn Sokol

Dance to the music; educate yourself. RasTa Time.

©Mitsuhiro Sugawara

EPILOGUE

"Now is Rasta's time."
Al Campbell

In these past years of negotiating this book's agreements, contracts and permissions, the promise of *RasTa Time* seemed elusive. It was a period of enduring the "system," learning its rules, obtaining copyrights, awaiting approvals, including the Marley Foundation's blessings for the book's release.

My publishing contract arrived on March 10, 2020, exactly nine years to the day from my departure from Japan to embark on this journey of interviewing Bob Marley's family and friends; just a day before Japan's great tragedies – the earthquakes, the tsunami, the radioactive desolation.

Now with my contract signed and sent, we are facing the greatest pandemic of the modern era. The world is in lockdown.

Bracketed by these calamities, I wonder if time has indeed "caught up with us," indeed, whether "our time is up."

Why do so many have to suffer and die as Bob sings in *Natural Mystic*?

According to Reggae's premier historian and archivist Roger Steffens, or Ras Rojah as Bob called him:

"Bob sang of the last days, which was kind of frightening because these do feel like the last days. I mean, the planet itself is rebelling against the infestation of humanity and Bob was sounding the horn and warning us all.

"I think Bob's greatest message was that in order to heal the world, you must heal yourself first, and it will radiate outward. So the work that has to be done is internal and an external demonstration of the one love vibration.

"It is so old it is cliché. All you need is love sang the Beatles. Love is the answer is an old Alton Ellis title. If you can't love and heal yourself, then the world is not going to be a better place.

RasTa Time

The work has to be done individually, one at a time. Everybody whose lives were touched by Bob was changed. There is not a doubt in my mind that this man was god-sent and his work will live forever. It's life-saving and life-savoring music."

How prescient are Ras Rojah's words, which I had the privilege of listening to as we sat in his L.A. home, talking and going through his archive, the world's most extensive collection of Reggae memorabilia. Steffens had hosted Santa Monica's pioneering FM radio program, *Reggae Beat*, and presented Bob Marley as his first guest. Starting in 1979, for 1400 hours across 400 Sundays, he played reggae and nothing but reggae. He released the first edition of *The Reggae Beat* magazine, now known as *Beat,* in 1982; the first edition given out free at his Second Annual Bob Marley Day in MacArthur Park on May 11th. Even today the magazine is read and sold worldwide.

Courtesy Roger Steffens

RasTa Time

Ras Rojah is a self-proclaimed Rasta evangelist.

"Everyone needs to know about Bob's life and to understand his seriousness of his purpose. Bob told me 'Reggae is not for jollifcation, it is for head-ucation,' and tapped his forehead when he said that.

"We are a part of a small group of people who have seen the light and seen how delightful your life can be when you see this particular reggae-fied, rasta-fied light. And we want to tell everybody we love about it and just spread the message. The message is one love. It is so simple but so hard. One love. One heart. Let's get together and be all right."

Will we be all right?

Our fate today may be unknown, but for some, not unforeseen. Many believe Bob Marley spoke prophetic wisdom. To me, he spoke at length of the last days.

"You can't stop it. Everything is in prophecy. This is the generation that see God... That mean over the whole earth. This generation of people seek the truth. That is what is happening right now. No

government or no nuclear weapon nor nothing at all can stop it.

You see when one ready, there's a lot of people whose ready. But this revolution will not be televised, it will be telepathic, you know.

… This is the last days…

All illusion. Madness. You have to burn everything. I mean, it shall be a new world. Cause this world shall be passed away."

If and when it is over, what is left but spirit?

One thing of which I am certain, Bob's spirit has followed me throughout my adult life. He appears to me in the most unexpected places. One night, on a friend's rooftop in Delhi dancing to Bob Marley's music, his shadowy image materialized on the stone wall of the neighboring house.

RasTa Time

While in Goa, walking down the street, along comes Bob to greet me.

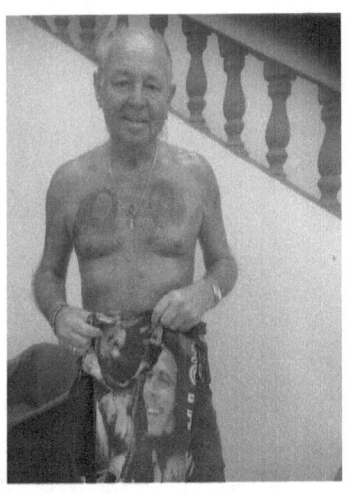

Bob's spirit definitely followed me in my pursuit for photos of Mrs. Rita Marley, the last hurdle that I faced for *RasTa Time's* publication.

I reached out to Patricia Scarlett, Donisha Prendergast's mentor and agent, who soon sent me the contact information for Michael Chambers, shown in this photograph with Donisha and her mother, Sharon.

Courtesy Michael Chambers

I first spoke with Michael on a misty morning in the mountains of Kyoto, and indeed, it was a mystical meeting. His disembodied voice over the phone, generated immediate trust, much like the trust that Bob Marley engendered when we first met backstage after the concert.

RasTa Time

Michael told me that just before I called he had found a photo of him and Mrs. Marley, taken in 2008 at the Bob Marley Museum, which he had not seen for years.

Kathy Arlyn Sokol

Courtesy Michael Chambers

She had had such an influence on him, Michael continued, that his image of himself as a photographer was forever changed. "Please don't call this a photo shoot," she had admonished him. "Your camera is not a weapon that 'shoots,' it is a tool for your creativity."

He then told her that during this 'session,' he would take a photo of her that would reveal her inner and outer beauty. The photo taken by Michael on that day is used as the profile photo for the Rita Marley interview and has now become her favorite picture of herself.

RasTa Time

Courtesy Michael Chambers

It has been more than forty years since I recorded Bob Marley's words, and I have listened to them over and over and over again. They have given shape to my reality.

My eternal gratitude to Bob Marley for a personal introduction to the realm of spirit; the realm that he inhabits here and now, and beyond…

Bob had requested at the end of our interview that I "do the right thing" with it, and *RasTa Time*, I know is the "right thing."

Kathy Arlyn Sokol

©*Mitsuhiro Sugawara*

ACKNOWLEDGEMENTS

The simple appreciative mention of the following individuals in no way fully expresses my abiding indebtedness and gratitude for their vital contributions to this work. Each play a distinctive role in RasTa Time's becoming and uniquely enriched my life.

Special Acknowledgments:

Terumaro Hiramoto, founder ALC
Ayumu Takahashi, publisher Factory A-Works
Ryo Ijichi, project producer
Kazimierex Kailash Kubiak, provider
Sugimoto Sugawara, esteemed photographer
Robert Brady, master wordsmith
Donisha Prendergast, Queen of RasTa
Gladstone "Gilly Dread" Gilbert, my guide
Asa M. Star Sokol-Kubiak, daughter supreme
Hideki Nakagawa, reggae-world connector
Michael Chambers, eminent photographer
    https://mchambers.smugmug.com/
W. David Kubiak, partner in Life

Kathy Arlyn Sokol

<u>Invaluable Support & Guidance:</u>

Alex Kerr
Alfonso D'Niscio Brooks
Alford Calman Scott
Ambassador Cynthia Barnes
Chris Blackwell
Dezi Catarino
Chris Case
Radha Case
Doreen Crujeiras
Jerry Riley
John Bour & Villa du Lac
Jonathan Demme
Katsu Geiko & the Hasegawa House
Rita Dixit-Kubiak
Gerald H. Sokol
Robert Sokol
Marlene Sokol-Stewart
Sandra Sokol Knight
Stomu Yamash'ta
Youhei Takimoto

RasTa Time

Graphic contributions:

Michael Hofmann
Ashlee Hutchinson
Jamaica Gleaner
King Sporty & Family
Faith Kubiak
Che Kothari
Jack Low, rasjack12@hotmail.com
Shin Miyoshi
Patricia Scarlett
Roger Steffens
Valzarok Creative Commons Wikipedia
Gail Zucker
Caribbean National Weekly

Sound engineers:

Haruki Oshindai
Tadashi Kondo
Ichiro Yoshida